T0301956

An Analysis of

David Brion Davis's

The Problem of Slavery in the Age of Revolution, 1770–1823

Duncan Money
with
Jason Xidias

Published by Macat International Ltd
24:13 Coda Centre, 189 Munster Road, London SW6 6AW.

Distributed exclusively by Routledge
2 Park Square, Milton Park, Abingdon, Oxon OX14 4RN
711 Third Avenue, New York, NY 10017, USA

Routledge is an imprint of the Taylor & Francis Group, an informa business

Copyright © 2017 by Macat International Ltd
Macat International has asserted its right under the Copyright, Designs and Patents Act
1988 to be identified as the copyright holder of this work.

The print publication is protected by copyright. Prior to any prohibited reproduction, storage in a
retrieval system, distribution or transmission in any form or by any means, electronic, mechanical,
recording or otherwise, permission should be obtained from the publisher or where applicable a
license permitting restricted copying in the United Kingdom should be obtained from the Copyright
Licensing Agency Ltd, Barnard's Inn, 86 Fetter Lane, London EC4A 1EN, UK.

The ePublication is protected by copyright and must not be copied, reproduced, transferred,
distributed, leased, licensed or publicly performed or used in any way except as specifically
permitted in writing by the publishers, as allowed under the terms and conditions under which it
was purchased, or as strictly permitted by applicable copyright law. Any unauthorised distribution
or use of this text may be a direct infringement of the authors and the publishers' rights and those
responsible may be liable in law accordingly.

www.macat.com
info@macat.com

Cataloguing in Publication Data
A catalogue record for this book is available from the British Library.
Library of Congress Cataloguing-in-Publication Data is available upon request.
Cover illustration: Etienne Gilfillan

ISBN 978-1-912302-48-2 (hardback)
ISBN 978-1-912128-16-7 (paperback)
ISBN 978-1-912281-36-7 (e-book)

Notice
The information in this book is designed to orientate readers of the work under analysis,
to elucidate and contextualise its key ideas and themes, and to aid in the development
of critical thinking skills. It is not meant to be used, nor should it be used, as a
substitute for original thinking or in place of original writing or research. References and
notes are provided for informational purposes and their presence does not constitute
endorsement of the information or opinions therein. This book is presented solely for
educational purposes. It is sold on the understanding that the publisher is not engaged
to provide any scholarly advice. The publisher has made every effort to ensure that
this book is accurate and up-to-date, but makes no warranties or representations with
regard to the completeness or reliability of the information it contains. The information
and the opinions provided herein are not guaranteed or warranted to produce particular
results and may not be suitable for students of every ability. The publisher shall not be
liable for any loss, damage or disruption arising from any errors or omissions, or from
the use of this book, including, but not limited to, special, incidental, consequential or
other damages caused, or alleged to have been caused, directly or indirectly, by the
information contained within.

CONTENTS

THE MACAT LIBRARY

The Macat Library is a series of unique academic explorations of seminal works in the humanities and social sciences – books and papers that have had a significant and widely recognised impact on their disciplines. It has been created to serve as much more than just a summary of what lies between the covers of a great book. It illuminates and explores the influences on, ideas of, and impact of that book. Our goal is to offer a learning resource that encourages critical thinking and fosters a better, deeper understanding of important ideas.

Each publication is divided into three Sections: Influences, Ideas, and Impact. Each Section has four Modules. These explore every important facet of the work, and the responses to it.

This Section-Module structure makes a Macat Library book easy to use, but it has another important feature. Because each Macat book is written to the same format, it is possible (and encouraged!) to cross-reference multiple Macat books along the same lines of inquiry or research. This allows the reader to open up interesting interdisciplinary pathways.

To further aid your reading, lists of glossary terms and people mentioned are included at the end of this book (these are indicated by an asterisk [*] throughout) – as well as a list of works cited.

Macat has worked with the University of Cambridge to identify the elements of critical thinking and understand the ways in which six different skills combine to enable effective thinking.
Three allow us to fully understand a problem; three more give us the tools to solve it. Together, these six skills make up the **PACIER** model of critical thinking. They are:

ANALYSIS – understanding how an argument is built
EVALUATION – exploring the strengths and weaknesses of an argument
INTERPRETATION – understanding issues of meaning

CREATIVE THINKING – coming up with new ideas and fresh connections
PROBLEM-SOLVING – producing strong solutions
REASONING – creating strong arguments

To find out more, visit **WWW.MACAT.COM.**

CRITICAL THINKING AND *THE PROBLEM OF SLAVERY IN THE AGE OF REVOLUTION*

Primary critical thinking skill: ANALYSIS
Secondary critical thinking skill: PROBLEM-SOLVING

How was it possible for opponents of slavery to be so vocal in opposing the practice, when they were so accepting of the economic exploitation of workers in western factories – many of which were owned by prominent abolitionists? David Brion Davis's *The Problem of Slavery in the Age of Revolution, 1770-1823*, uses the critical thinking skill of analysis to break down the various arguments that were used to condemn one set of controversial practices, and examine those that were used to defend another. His study allows us to see clear differences in reasoning and to test the assumptions made by each argument in turn.

The result is an eye-opening explanation that makes it clear exactly how contemporaries resolved this apparent dichotomy – one that allows us to judge whether the opponents of slavery were clear-eyed idealists, or simply deployers of arguments that pandered to their own base economic interests.

ABOUT THE AUTHOR OF THE ORIGINAL WORK

David Brion Davis is an American historian, acclaimed for his work on
the history of slavery and abolition. Born in 1927, he was drafted into the
American army in 1945, where he witnessed white army officers
discriminating against black troops. Studying American History at Harvard
University later in life, Davis started reading about slavery. Realizing how
profoundly slavery had influenced Western life, he was shocked by the lack
of research on the subject, and has since devoted his career to changing
that state of affairs.

ABOUT THE AUTHORS OF THE ANALYSIS

Dr Duncan Money holds a DPhil in history from the University of
Oxford for research focusing on mining in the African copper belt. He is
currently a Postdoctoral Research Fellow at the International Studies
Group, University of the Free State in South Africa.

Dr Jason Xidias holds a PhD in European Politics from King's College
London, where he completed a comparative dissertation on immigration
and citizenship in Britain and France. He was also a Visiting Fellow in
European Politics at the University of California, Berkeley. Currently, he is
Lecturer in Political Science at New York University.

ABOUT MACAT

GREAT WORKS FOR CRITICAL THINKING

Macat is focused on making the ideas of the world's great thinkers
accessible and comprehensible to everybody, everywhere, in ways that
promote the development of enhanced critical thinking skills.

It works with leading academics from the world's top universities to
produce new analyses that focus on the ideas and the impact of the most
influential works ever written across a wide variety of academic disciplines.
Each of the works that sit at the heart of its growing library is an enduring
example of great thinking. But by setting them in context – and looking
at the influences that shaped their authors, as well as the responses they
provoked – Macat encourages readers to look at these classics and
game-changers with fresh eyes. Readers learn to think, engage and
challenge their ideas, rather than simply accepting them.

'Macat offers an amazing first-of-its-kind tool for interdisciplinary learning and research. Its focus on works that transformed their disciplines and its rigorous approach, drawing on the world's leading experts and educational institutions, opens up a world-class education to anyone.'

Andreas Schleicher
Director for Education and Skills, Organisation for Economic
Co-operation and Development

'Macat is taking on some of the major challenges in university education … They have drawn together a strong team of active academics who are producing teaching materials that are novel in the breadth of their approach.'

Prof Lord Broers,
former Vice-Chancellor of the University of Cambridge

'The Macat vision is exceptionally exciting. It focuses upon new modes of learning which analyse and explain seminal texts which have profoundly influenced world thinking and so social and economic development. It promotes the kind of critical thinking which is essential for any society and economy.
This is the learning of the future.'

Rt Hon Charles Clarke, former UK Secretary of State for Education

'The Macat analyses provide immediate access to the critical conversation surrounding the books that have shaped their respective discipline, which will make them an invaluable resource to all of those, students and teachers, working in the field.'

Professor William Tronzo, University of California at San Diego

WAYS IN TO THE TEXT

KEY POINTS

- David Brion Davis is Professor Emeritus at Yale University. He is widely regarded as an eminent historian on slavery and antislavery.

- Written in 1975, *The Problem of Slavery in the Age of Revolution, 1770–1823* tells the story of slavery, antislavery, and the process by which slavery was outlawed in America and Britain.

- *The Problem of Slavery in the Age of Revolution, 1770–1823* changed our understanding of history. It remains an important reference point for the social sciences.

Who Is David Brion Davis?

David Brion Davis is the American author of *The Problem of Slavery in the Age of Revolution, 1770–1823*. Widely recognized as one of the foremost scholars of slavery and abolitionism* (the movement to end slavery), he is one of the most eminent historians of his generation.

Davis was born in the American city of Denver in the state of Colorado in 1927. Due to his father's work as a journalist, the family moved frequently, living in California, New York, Washington State, and Colorado. Then, in June 1945, when Davis was 18, he was drafted into the American army and sent to serve in occupied Germany. This experience was to shape his future career. Davis witnessed repeated discrimination by white army officers against the black troops. He found this exposure to the realities of racial prejudice deeply disturbing.

Davis returned to the United States, where he studied philosophy at Dartmouth College; he later completed a PhD in American History at Harvard University. Reading about slavery and antislavery there, he quickly came to realize that the subject had been under-researched. Davis made it his goal to increase scholarly and public understanding of the practice of slavery. He studied why it had happened as well as why, in the late eighteenth century, campaigners had called for its abolition.

First at Cornell University and then at Yale, Davis has spent his academic career researching and writing about slavery and antislavery. The author and editor of 17 books and a recipient of the prestigious Pulitzer Prize,* awarded for excellence in journalism, music, and literature, he retired from full-time teaching in 2001. Today, he is Sterling Professor of History Emeritus and Director Emeritus of the Gilder Lehrman Center for the Study of Slavery, Resistance, and Abolition.

What Does *The Problem of Slavery in the Age of Revolution* Say?

Written in 1975, Davis's *The Problem of Slavery in the Age of Revolution* is the second book in a trilogy about slavery in the West, coming after *The Problem of Slavery in Western Culture* (1966). Both books were written with the following two aims: Davis wanted to contribute to academic debates on slavery, and he wanted to address the fact that slavery was rarely taught in American and British schools.

Davis's books show that people in the West had ignored the horrific institution of slavery since the beginning of recorded history. The ideology and practice of slavery had been justified in Christian doctrine and in Western philosophy for centuries. Davis asks why this changed.

Why, in other words, did a profound shift in attitudes towards slavery occur in the eighteenth and early nineteenth centuries?

Previous scholars had argued that Britain abolished slavery in the Caribbean because its economic interests there had changed. Other scholars attributed the end of slavery to abolitionist struggles, without looking at the wider context for these events. Davis thought that these explanations for the antislavery movement were too simplistic. He wanted to provide a deeper analysis.

In *The Problem of Slavery in the Age of Revolution*, he says it is important to make a clear separation between two related aspects of the antislavery movement:
- The origins of antislavery ideas
- The development of the movements they inspired.
- This leads to another distinction, between:
- The people who first argued that slavery was morally wrong
- The people who took practical action to end slavery.

Davis argues that antislavery developed in different ways in different countries due to distinct national values and the differences between the various groups that supported abolition. To explore this idea, he compares slavery and antislavery in Britain, America, and France.

Davis's most influential ideas relate to the British antislavery movement. He argues that abolition served the needs of Britain's governing elite.

Davis believed that the rise of the antislavery movement was intimately linked to the development of the economic system of capitalism,* in which things such as land, technology, and resources are held in private hands, and which brought with it new forms of oppression, such as worker exploitation, child labor, and poverty. Davis argues that the crusade to end slavery in the British Empire diverted attention away from the harsh conditions of capitalism.

Antislavery served the class interest of the British elite. As a result, the British elite supported it.

The situation in America was different. Americans emphasized the concepts of liberty and equality for all. There were strong abolitionist movements in the North and South of the country, but despite America's revolutionary ideals, the ruling classes fiercely resisted abolishing slavery.

The French experience was different again. In France, slaves had been emancipated during the French Revolution* but they were re-enslaved by Napoleon* and did not regain their freedom for another half-century.

The Problem of Slavery in the Age of Revolution reveals the complexity of antislavery. The book points out the contradictions of the movement. But Davis also celebrates it. He sees abolition as a remarkable achievement and a milestone in human progress.

Why Does *The Problem of Slavery in the Age of Revolution* Matter?

Davis is one of the most eminent historians of his generation. He has inspired a generation of scholars through his teaching and writing. *The Problem of Slavery in the Age of Revolution*, published in 1975, is one of his most important books, the second text in a trilogy. The first volume, *The Problem of Slavery in Western Culture*, was published in 1966. The final volume, *The Problem of Slavery in the Age of Emancipation*, was published in 2014.

Before these books were written, Davis had identified a gap in the scholarly literature on slavery. Teachers, historians, and others in the West had largely ignored their countries' histories of slavery, antislavery, and abolition. So Davis's trilogy was written for anyone interested in these subjects. It's also a rewarding read for anyone interested more broadly in American and British history.

To write his books, Davis carried out a meticulous analysis of the archival sources on slavery. In *The Problem of Slavery in Western Culture*, he explores the centuries in which the practice of slavery was justified both theologically (that is, with reference to Christian texts) and philosophically in Western societies. In *The Problem of Slavery in the Age of Revolution* he looks at the dramatic rise of antislavery—a movement formed by people who were determined to eradicate this practice. The book provides a comparative analysis of early antislavery movements and discusses the controversies over slavery.

These controversies shaped changes in national attitudes towards labor, social order, and political representation (the means by which the voices of citizens are heard in their government).

Although the book's primary focus is on slavery and antislavery in British and American territories, the author also provides valuable insights into the history of slavery in France and Latin America.

Acclaimed by other historians, *The Problem of Slavery in the Age of Revolution* won awards in America such as the National Book Award, the Albert J. Beveridge Award, and the Bancroft Prize, as well as others overseas. It has inspired volumes of further research on slavery and antislavery in history. Davis's work has also led to greater understanding of these issues among the public. Used regularly as a point of reference by historians, *The Problem of Slavery in the Age of Revolution* will remain a central text for future work in this field.

SECTION 1
INFLUENCES

MODULE 1
THE AUTHOR AND THE HISTORICAL CONTEXT

KEY POINTS

- The text is essential reading for anyone working on the history of slavery, antislavery, and abolitionism* (the movement dedicated to the ending of slavery) and American or British history.

- While completing his PhD, Davis identified an important gap in scholarly literature on the history of slavery and antislavery. He addressed this throughout his academic career.

- *The Problem of Slavery in the Age of Revolution* is the sequel to Davis's earlier work, *The Problem of Slavery in Western Culture*.

Why Read This Text?

David Brion Davis's prize-winning text *The Problem of Slavery in the Age of Revolution, 1770–1823* (1975) is an essential book for anyone working on the history of slavery, antislavery, and abolitionism. It is also a key text for anyone interested in American or British history. The first sequel to the author's earlier work *The Problem of Slavery in Western Culture* (1966), the book provides a compelling and influential account of the emergence of the antislavery movement in Britain and the United States.

Davis seeks to explain why, after slavery had been accepted in Western societies for centuries, a movement suddenly arose calling for it to be abolished. He offers an innovative and compelling account of the relationship between social change, moral change, and political action.

❝ David Brion Davis has spent a lifetime contemplating the worst of humanity and the best of humanity—the terrible cruelty and injustice of slavery, perpetuated over centuries and across borders and oceans, overturned at last because of ideas and ideals given substance through human action and human agency. **❞**

Drew Gilpin Faust,* "The Scholar Who Shaped History"

In *The Problem of Slavery in Western Culture*, Davis had explored Western ideas about slavery, looking back over two thousand years of history. He built on this in *The Problem of Slavery in the Age of Revolution*, looking at the ideas that led to the revolutions in America (1775–83), France (1789–99), and Haiti (1791–1804).

Davis explains how the rise of an antislavery doctrine led to the abolition of slavery in England. He looks at the creation of Haiti as the world's first black republic, the gradual end of the slave trade* across the Atlantic (the selling of black Africans to slavery in the Americas), and the abolition of slavery in the American North. He also highlights the great challenges that abolitionists faced. The planter class*—made up of the slave owners in the American South—was closely associated with (and in some cases was part of) the governments of England, France, and America. Furthermore, slave labor was essential to industrialization* (the process by which tasks formerly performed by manual labor are mechanized, bringing an end to economies based on agriculture) and the accumulation of capital (roughly, wealth used for investment in the expectation of profit) in Europe and the United States.

Author's Life

Davis was born into a literary family in the American city of Denver, Colorado, in 1927. His father was a journalist and novelist, and his mother a writer and painter. His father's work meant that the family moved from one part of the United States to another, including periods spent in the states of California, New York, Washington, and Colorado.

His education took a meandering path towards history. He studied philosophy at Dartmouth College, an American university where he obtained a Bachelor of Arts degree in 1950. Then he took courses in creative writing, and contemplated becoming a scientist or a journalist before undertaking postgraduate work at Harvard University, studying American history and earning a PhD in 1956. It was at Harvard that he became aware of the gap in scholarly literature with regard to slavery. He also realized how deficient his own education had been in this respect.

After completing his PhD, Davis worked as a professor at Cornell University and then at Yale University, where today he is Sterling Professor of History Emeritus and Director Emeritus of the Gilder Lehrman Center for the Study of Slavery, Resistance, and Abolition.

He has authored and edited 17 books. In 2014, US President Barack Obama* presented him with the National Humanities Medal for his great contribution to our understanding of history.

Author's Background

As Davis began his academic career, the American civil rights movement*—the struggle of black Americans and their allies to end discrimination—was becoming increasingly prominent. Anti-colonial struggles were being waged in Africa and Asia, while Europe was experiencing substantial post-war immigration, with newcomers arriving from former European colonies. Like the black population in America, these immigrants would confront discrimination and exploitation.

Davis had already seen for himself the sharp racial divisions in American society. As an infantryman serving in the US Army in the aftermath of World War II,* he had witnessed the hostility between white and black troops. He notes that the closest he came to combat was during a confrontation between black and white American troops outside a bar in the German city of Mannheim.[1]

The racial tension was even noticeable on the voyage over to Europe. On a troop ship Davis was shocked to find there were two thousand black soldiers kept beneath deck in conditions he compares to those of a slave ship.[2] He was equipped with a club and instructed to go down there to prevent them from gambling. Reflecting on these experiences in the year 2000, Davis noted: "I strongly suspect that this experience in Germany influenced my later decision to devote over forty years to the study of slavery and race."[3]

Two decades after the war, his first book on slavery was published: the Pulitzer Prize–winning *The Problem of Slavery in Western Culture.*[4] This, along with his position as an established academic at Yale, the prestigious American university, ensured that Davis had the funding and opportunities to consult sources at libraries and archives across the United States, Britain, France, and the Caribbean. This allowed him to carry out the meticulous research necessary for the project's success.

NOTES

1 David Brion Davis, "World War II and Memory," *The Journal of American History* 77, no. 2 (September 1990): 580.

2 Davis, "World War II," 582.

3 David Brion Davis, "The Americanized Mannheim of 1945–1946," in *American Places: Encounters with History: A Celebration of Sheldon Meyer*, ed. William Leuchtenburg (Oxford: Oxford University Press, 2000), 91.

4 David Brion Davis, *The Problem of Slavery in Western Culture* (Ithaca: Cornell University Press, 1966).

MODULE 2
ACADEMIC CONTEXT

KEY POINTS

- Davis addressed the complex relationship between capitalism* (the economic system in which a laborer's "tools" belong to those who profit from the labor they perform), slavery, and abolitionism* (the movement to end slavery).

- Previous scholars had attributed the end of slavery either to shifting British economic interests or to the progressive ideals of abolitionists.

- In the text, Davis sought to deepen understanding about why and how abolition occurred when it did.

The Work in its Context

David Brion Davis's *The Problem of Slavery in the Age of Revolution* was the sequel to his earlier work *The Problem of Slavery in Western Culture.*[1] The success of his first book had sparked greater academic interest in the history of both slavery and antislavery. As a result, *Slavery in the Age of Revolution* (1975) was one of several important academic works on these subjects published in the mid-1970s. Others included the American historian Seymour Drescher's* *Econocide*[2] and the British historian Roger Anstey's* *The Atlantic Slave Trade and British Abolition.*[3] In his 1975 text, Davis focused on the relationship between capitalism and the abolition of slavery.

In 1944, the historian Eric Williams,* who was also the prime minister of the Caribbean nation of Trinidad and Tobago, had made a major contribution to the debate on these subjects by publishing his book *Capitalism and Slavery.*[4] In it he argued that economic

❝ The new hostility to human bondage cannot be reduced simply to the needs and interests of particular classes. Yet the needs and interests of particular classes had much to do with a given society's receptivity to new ideas and thus to the ideas' historical impact. ❞

David Brion Davis, *The Problem of Slavery in the Age of Revolution, 1770–1823*

considerations had led to Britain ending slavery in its Caribbean colonies. Previous scholars had attributed this action to the social struggles of abolitionists, but Williams argued that it was due to economic decline in Britain's Caribbean colonies. Coupled with the rising power of industrial capitalists in Britain, this prompted a shift in the country's economic strategy, with slavery coming to be seen as an inefficient system.

However, many historians, including Davis, viewed this account as being too simplistic. Davis himself pointed to evidence that suggested that the Caribbean slave colonies were not in decline. However, he also argued that it was important to account for the broader economic context in which slavery was abolished, rather than giving all the credit to the progressive ideals of abolitionists.

Overview of the Field

By the early 1970s—when Davis was researching and writing *The Problem of Slavery in the Age of Revolution*—the American civil rights movement* (the collective name for the organizations and individuals fighting for an end to discrimination against black Americans) had sparked a debate over the continuing marginalization of African Americans in American society.

One question concerned how this discrimination had originated. Most ancestors of the black American population were in America because of the Atlantic slave trade.* They had, in other words, been forcibly taken to the United States and sold as slaves. This history provided a crucial context for the discrimination and disadvantages faced by African Americans in the 1970s.

Although Davis did not draw the parallel himself, it is true that the abolitionist* movement had visible similarities to the civil rights movement. Both drew inspiration from Christian theology and scripture and were motivated by a resolute desire to address racially based discrimination. These parallels meant that Davis's book spoke clearly to most of the population making up contemporary American society.

In both *Age of Revolution* and its predecessor, *The Problem of Slavery in Western Culture*, Davis sought to fill a gap in US historiography* (that is, in the written works dealing with American history) and to encourage greater academic interest in slavery and antislavery. Both books were enormously successful in meeting these aims and are widely seen as foundational texts in this field.

Academic Influences

When Davis was a doctoral student at Harvard University, slavery occupied a very marginal position in the curriculum. It was not even mentioned in major historical works on eighteenth- and nineteenth-century American history.

During his studies though, Davis came across Swedish economist Gunnar Myrdal's* book *An American Dilemma* (1944),[5] a text that had a significant impact on him. Myrdal argued that if segregation were overturned and black people were granted equal legal citizenship, America could solve its problem of racism. Years later, in 1992, Davis responded to this claim in a press article titled "The American Dilemma." In it, he argued that equal legal citizenship was insufficient for America to overcome its "pathology of race." To do so it would have to confront its "destructive myth of a classless society."[6]

The American historian Kenneth Stampp* was another important influence on Davis. The two talked in the 1950s, while Stampp was in the process of completing a major work on slavery, his book *The Peculiar Institution: Slavery in the Ante-Bellum South* (1956).[7] "In talking with Ken about this enormously important subject," Davis wrote, "he made me realize that it had been marginalized and virtually erased in the courses I'd had at Harvard and as an undergraduate at Dartmouth."[8]

NOTES

1   David Brion Davis, *The Problem of Slavery in Western Culture* (Ithaca: Cornell University Press, 1966).

2   Seymour Drescher, *Econocide: British Slavery in the Era of Abolition* (Pittsburgh: Pittsburgh University Press, 1977).

3   Roger Anstey, *The Atlantic Slave Trade and British Abolition, 1760–1810* (London: Macmillan, 1975).

4   Eric Williams, *Capitalism and Slavery* (Chapel Hill: University of North Carolina Press, 1944).

5   Gunnar Myrdal, *An American Dilemma: The Negro Problem and Modern Democracy* (New York: Harper & Brothers, 1944).

6   David Brion Davis, "The American Dilemma," *The New York Review of Books*, July 16, 1992.

7   Kenneth Stampp, *A Peculiar Institution: Slavery in the Ante-Bellum South* (New York: Alfred A. Knopf, 1956).

8   Donald A. Yerxa, "On Slavery and Antislavery: An Interview with David Brion Davis," *Historically Speaking* (July–August 2007).

MODULE 3
THE PROBLEM

KEY POINTS

- Davis's core theme is the relationship between the economic system of capitalism* and the antislavery movements.

- Davis argued that shifting economic interest is too simple an explanation for the British abolition of slavery in the Caribbean.

- Davis argued that Britain's emergent capitalist class used the antislavery movement to expand its economic interests.

Core Question

In *The Problem of Slavery in the Age of Revolution, 1770–1823*, David Brion Davis seeks to explain the relationship between capitalism and the antislavery movements. This had only been addressed superficially in previous scholarly literature. Davis looked for an answer in the context of the major economic and political changes that occurred during what he labels the "Age of Revolution,"* between 1770 and 1823—a period of war, political and economic upheaval, and antislavery movements.

Davis sought to address two key questions:

- In what ways did the economic and political forces of this time either undermine or strengthen slavery in the Americas?
- How did shifts in economic, political, and military power help shape the moral condemnation of slavery?

❝ The key questions concern the relationship between antislavery and the social system as a whole. Why did a seemingly liberal movement emerge and continue to win support from major government leaders in the period from 1790 to 1832, a period characterized by both political reaction and industrial revolution? … How could antislavery help ensure stability while also accommodating society to political and economic change? ❞

David Brion Davis, *The Problem of Slavery in the Age of Revolution, 1770–1823*

When Davis's book was published, these issues seemed of great relevance to contemporary Western society. The United States and many European countries had experienced major transformations during the 1950s and 1960s. Among the key events that had shaped these were the civil rights movement* (dedicated to the end of racial discrimination in the United States), anti-colonial struggles against former colonial powers in Africa and Asia, and post-war immigration into Europe by people from the continent's former colonies. These events shed light on the huge amount of discrimination and exploitation that blacks had faced, and continued to face, in the West.

The Participants

Davis was not the first historian to explore the relationship between the rise of capitalism and the development of mass antislavery movements. Many other historians had also argued that these developments were somehow linked. But Davis's approach to the question was quite novel.

He started by outlining the long history of the acceptance of slavery in the West. In showing that slavery dated back to ancient times, the author demonstrates why the emergence of the antislavery movement is so puzzling. Both Britain and America were heavily involved in the slave trade, and it was a practice that was deeply embedded in the psychology and social structures of these societies. This, said Davis, made them unlikely locations for antislavery movements to arise among their people.[1]

The success of the antislavery movement in Britain seems particularly puzzling. In Britain during the period in question (1770–1823), economic and political elites were hostile to the idea of social change. That hostility hardened in the aftermath of the French Revolution.* Also in Britain, moreover, many social evils were associated with the Industrial Revolution,* when labor was mechanized on a large scale, changing the economy and society in very widespread and significant ways. It is not clear why the change in moral perception produced such an intense focus on slavery, rather than on other issues.

Davis offers answers to these questions by looking at how the ideology* of antislavery intersected with the ideas and needs of an emerging capitalist class. He argues that taking a stance against free labor (slavery) helped to protect and cement the interests of capitalism during a time of great social and political change.

The Contemporary Debate

One of the strands of Davis's argument in *Age of Revolution* is a response to the Caribbean historian Eric Williams's* argument that economic decline in the Caribbean led to the end of slavery there. Davis claims that "economic trends do not explain the politics of British abolition,"[2] and criticizes Williams for "naïve determinism"[3] (that is, a rather shallow understanding of causes and effects whereby the actions of individuals are wrongly linked to certain events).

Davis also argues against those academics, such as the British historian Roger Anstey,* who said that the abolitionists' political arguments and actions, favoring social reform, were the primary motivation for the end of slavery. Anstey argued that the abolition of the slave trade occurred because, following the death of the British prime minister William Pitt* in January 1806, the majority of the government was convinced of the rightness of the cause.[4]

Davis offers an alternative interpretation: he argues that an antislavery ideology supported the interests of an emergent capitalist class. By attacking slave labor, industrialists were able to legitimize the more modern and acceptable system of capitalism. Low wages could be seen as a morally superior alternative to slavery.

Wages, which the industrialists portrayed as a concession to political and social struggles, became a symbol of freedom. This diverted attention away from the harsh realities of capitalism, such as continued worker exploitation in factories and child labor.

NOTES

1   David Brion Davis, *The Problem of Slavery in the Age of Revolution,* (Ithaca: Cornell University Press, 1975), 84.

2   Davis, *Age of Revolution,* 56.

3   Davis, *Age of Revolution*, 348.

4   Roger Anstey, "Capitalism and Slavery, a Critique," *The Economic History Review* 21, no. 2 (August 1968): 315.

MODULE 4
THE AUTHOR'S CONTRIBUTION

KEY POINTS

- Davis believed that previous scholarly accounts of slavery and antislavery were too simplistic.

- *The Problem of Slavery in the Age of Revolution* provides a detailed account of British antislavery. It explains why British elites accepted the abolition of slavery.

- His synthesis of the economic system of capitalism,* antislavery, and the social movement of abolitionism* made an original contribution to the field of history.

Author's Aims

David Brion Davis's book *The Problem of Slavery in the Age of Revolution, 1770–1823* was the sequel to an earlier work, *The Problem of Slavery in Western Culture.*[1] In this earlier work, Davis describes how, for centuries, writers and thinkers justified slavery on the grounds of theology (that is, by referencing Christian texts and scripture) and philosophy. He then outlines the transformation in Western thought: in the eighteenth century, for the first time, slavery faced a moral challenge.

In *The Problem of Slavery in the Age of Revolution*, Davis builds on this, explaining why this shift in moral attitudes occurred and why it focused on the evils of slavery, rather than on other pressing moral problems of the era under discussion.

Davis had initially hoped to use a wider comparative approach to the subject than just focusing on Britain and America. He'd intended to also look in depth at the antislavery movements in France and Latin America. One of the reasons he termed the period of 1770 to

> 66 If British abolitionists could express horror over the iron chains of the slave trade, their acts of selectivity and definition helped to strengthen the invisible chains being forged at home. Accusations of 'inconsistency' or 'hypocrisy' can only obscure the complex relationship between West Indian slavery and the more progressive thought of early industrial England. As reformers grappled with the problems of crime, pauperism, and labor discipline, they seemed to be unconsciously haunted by the image of the slave plantation. 99
>
> David Brion Davis, *The Problem of Slavery in the Age of Revolution, 1770–1823*

1823 the "Age of Revolution"* is that it was during this era that many nations in Latin America fought successfully for independence.[2]

This plan proved too ambitious, however. The final version of the book concentrates on antislavery in Britain and the United States, with some coverage of France this alone takes 564 pages. Given the level of detail in the work, a wider geographical analysis would probably have been impractical for a single volume.

Approach

Existing work on abolitionism tended to regard abolitionists in one of two ways. Some academics argued that abolitionists were humanitarians, selflessly motivated by the urge to eradicate a great social evil. Others argued that their idealistic attitudes masked base economic motives—which they claimed were the real driving force behind abolition. Davis tried to overcome this division between those who ascribed crude economic motives to abolitionism and those who put it down to enlightened idealism* (that is, the belief that some "ideal" state of affairs is achievable).

To do this, he carried out a detailed survey of the antislavery movements in the United States and Britain between 1770 and 1823. In this, he carefully distinguishes between the origin of antislavery ideas and the reasons why they were accepted by political and economic elites.

Referencing utilitarianism*—the belief that the "best" course of action is the one that makes the most people happy—Davis expresses his thesis as follows: "British antislavery helped to ensure stability while accommodating society to political and economic change; it merged Utilitarianism with an ethic of benevolence, reinforcing faith that a progressive policy of *laissez-faire** [that is, deliberate inaction] would reveal men's natural identity of interests. It opened new sources of moral prestige for the dominant social class … and looked forward to the universal goal of compliant, loyal, and self-disciplined workers."[3]

In other words, slavery was morally categorized as an unacceptable form of exploitation. This allowed political elites and industrial capitalists to pursue a modern, slightly less oppressive form of exploitation—that of wage labor* in factories.

This insight into the relationship between capitalism, antislavery, and abolition was an original contribution to the field.

Contribution in Context

After two millennia during which slavery was considered justifiable, "a profound transformation in moral perception" led many Europeans and Americans "to see the full horror of a social evil to which mankind had been blind for centuries."[4] In *The Problem of Slavery in the Age of Revolution* Davis explores the implications of this shift in moral perception.

One historical tradition, emphasized by nationalistic* British historians (that is, historians who believed in the superiority of British culture for political reasons), argued that the movement to abolish slavery was motivated by selfless idealistic concerns. It was a view supported by the British government for many of the same reasons.

Another historical tradition was associated with Marxist* historians (that is, historians who analyze historical events according to the economic and social theories proposed by Karl Marx*—a man who introduced a very radical critique of the social effects of capitalism). Of these, the Caribbean scholar Eric Williams* is particularly notable.

These Marxist historians saw ulterior economic motives behind antislavery rhetoric* and traced the rise of abolitionism to the declining importance of slavery within a British economy rapidly moving towards industrialization.* In contrast, Davis sought "a middle ground that rejects Williams's cynical reductionism* [that is, his tactical over-simplification] while also taking account of the realities of class power."[5]

Davis used his knowledge of the intellectual justifications for slavery to create a new thesis. He argued that early opponents of slavery were motivated by deeply held and religiously inspired beliefs about the evils of slavery, but that the acceptance of the movement, at least in Britain, can be attributed to the way in which it supported the needs of the emerging capitalist class and the new economic order.

NOTES

1   David Brion Davis, *The Problem of Slavery in Western Culture* (Ithaca: Cornell University Press, 1966).

2   David Brion Davis, *The Problem of Slavery in the Age of Revolution, 1770–1823* (Ithaca: Cornell University Press, 1975), 12.

3   Davis, *Age of Revolution,* 384–5.

4   Davis, *Age of Revolution*, 11.

5   David Brion Davis, "Reflections on Abolitionism and Ideological Hegemony," *The American Historical Review* 92, no. 4 (October 1987): 797.

SECTION 2
IDEAS

MODULE 5
MAIN IDEAS

KEY POINTS

- Davis addresses why British elites came to accept the abolition of slavery.

- One of the major themes of the work is the relationship between ideology and social structure.

- The link between capitalism* and the emergence of antislavery is one of the most distinctive arguments in the book.

Key Themes

In *The Problem of Slavery in the Age of Revolution 1770–1823*, David Brion Davis argues that the recognition of slavery as a social evil at the end of the eighteenth century and the beginning of the nineteenth was "a momentous turning point in the evolution of man's moral perception, and thus in man's image of himself."[1]

He shows how opposition to slavery developed during a period of dramatic political and economic upheaval, and addresses some of the specific religious and political developments that made antislavery a major issue in America and Britain. The book is an intellectual history of ideas and an account of how those ideas generated social change.

Davis places great weight on the role of a Christian movement called the Quakers.* The religious principles of the Quakers inspired—certainly in many who belonged to the sect—a deeply held desire to eradicate slavery. The discipline and organization of the Quakers helped them to popularize these ideas and foster a political movement in favor of abolition.[2]

❝ British antislavery helped to ensure stability while accommodating society to political and economic change; it merged Utilitarianism with an ethic of benevolence, reinforcing faith that a progressive policy of laissez faire would reveal men's natural identity of interests. It opened new sources of moral prestige for the dominant social class, helped to define a participatory role for middle-class activism, and looked forward to the universal goal of compliant, loyal, and self-disciplined workers. ❞

David Brion Davis, *The Problem of Slavery in the Age of Revolution, 1770–1823*

In the late eighteenth and early nineteenth centuries, however, the antislavery movement had greatly different outcomes in different countries. Davis looks at Britain and the United States separately, exploring the particular circumstances that explain the successes and failures of the antislavery movements in these countries.

Slavery played a crucial role in American society. Davis highlights the apparent paradox that "systematic violence and exploitation … underlay a society genuinely dedicated to individual freedom and equality of opportunity."[3] He then turns to Britain, where the abolitionist movement achieved comparative success. Davis emphasizes that the reason behind the social acceptance of antislavery ideas here was that abolition served the needs of the social and political elite, who wanted to expand capitalism while safeguarding their privileged position at a time of political and social struggle. Supporting abolition gave the elites moral credibility while diverting attention away from the inequalities of capitalism.

Exploring the Ideas

Davis is interested in "the ideological functions and implications" of the antislavery movement.[4] Believing that these functions and implications were very different in Britain from those in the United States, he treats both countries separately (although there is some degree of comparison in the book).

Davis discusses the moral and religious underpinnings of antislavery ideas. But, he notes, "these cultural transformations by no means explain, by themselves, the appearance of organized efforts to rid the world of slavery."[5]

The phenomenon that does explain the appearance of these organized efforts in Britain is, Davis believes, the development of industrial capitalism. The emergence of this economic system during the same period as the development of the antislavery sentiment is not, he argues, a coincidence. Capitalism created the conditions in which potentially radical antislavery ideals could be accepted.

Davis points out the paradox* that existed: while there were calls to rid the world of one form of oppression—slavery—another form, low-wage factory labor, was being introduced.

Antislavery provided the emerging commercial and industrial class with moral authority. At a time of great political and social opposition, it gave them a much-needed image of being benevolent and progressive. It allowed them to present the wage economy, however exploitative it was and however low the wages were, as a modern and acceptable form of labor simply because it was preferable to slavery.

This is the most significant idea in *Age of Revolution*. Davis points out that antislavery advocates did not set out to benefit capitalism as a deliberate point of strategy, but, as he notes, "the ideological meaning of a reform is something more than the sum of the reformers' motives and intentions."[6]

Antislavery, according to Davis, quickly came to reflect "the ideological needs of various groups and classes." This is a contentious idea. These "groups" included the Quakers, who, as well as being central to the antislavery movement, were heavily involved in commerce and industry; as such, they were part of the capitalist elite whose needs were served by abolition.

Language and Expression

One of the reasons why Davis's *The Problem of Slavery in the Age of Revolution* is such a significant work is that it outlines a general argument about the link between moral thought and social change in an accessible, clear, and meticulous manner.

Davis stressed in a response to some of the critics of *Age of Revolution* that the antislavery movements in Britain and the United States were "the initiative of unique individuals embedded in unique social situations." It is clear, however, that his argument has wider implications[7] about the way in which ideas are translated into political action and social change.

Rejecting the notion that ideas reflect direct material interests, Davis makes an important distinction between the *origins* of ideas and the reasons for their wider acceptance. He uses this distinction in *Age of Revolution* to explain why British elites endorsed antislavery while remaining silent about the exploitation and dire working conditions that were introduced during the Industrial Revolution.*

Antislavery ideals sprang from the religious beliefs of nonconformist* groups (that is, Christian groups that did not follow the practices and beliefs of the Church of England) and philosophers of the Enlightenment* (a seventeenth- and eighteenth-century European school of thought that emphasized reason over tradition and religion).

The arguments of the antislavery movement quickly came to play an important role in legitimizing wage labor. They also helped to create a vocabulary that described oppression and, in doing so, played down other forms of exploitation.

Davis stresses that antislavery advocates were not consciously advancing the interests of a particular class. They remained convinced that theirs was a humanitarian project. For Davis, this illustrates his argument about the "social functions of ideology." That is, individuals can pursue their class interests without intending to, all the while thinking they are doing the opposite.[8]

NOTES

1   David Brion Davis, *The Problem of Slavery in the Age of Revolution, 1770–1823* (Ithaca: Cornell University Press, 1975), 42.

2   Davis, *Age of Revolution*, 214–15.

3   Davis, *Age of Revolution*, 85.

4   Davis, *Age of Revolution,* 13.

5   Davis, *Age of Revolution*, 48.

6   Davis, *Age of Revolution*, 446.

7   David Brion Davis, "The Perils of Doing History by Ahistorical Abstraction," in *The Antislavery Debate: Capitalism and Abolitionism as a Problem in Historical Interpretation*, ed. Thomas Bender (Berkley: University of California Press, 1992), 270.

8   Davis, *Age of Revolution,* 350.

MODULE 6
SECONDARY IDEAS

KEY POINTS

- David Brion Davis explores the historical tension between natural rights*—those rights we are supposed to hold by the virtue of the fact that we exist—and private property in relation to political philosophy.

- He examines how slavery, antislavery, and abolition have evolved differently in America and Britain.

- These are both important themes that continue to have implications for the way these societies are organized.

Other Ideas

There are two key secondary themes in David Brion Davis's book *The Problem of Slavery in the Age of Revolution, 1770–1823.*

The first is the tension between natural rights and private property and how this is expressed in political philosophy; natural rights are those rights that, according to the eighteenth-century political philosopher Thomas Paine, belong to all of us by virtue of the fact that we exist.

There has always been a conflict between the idea of a slave as property and the recognition of the natural rights and humanity of the individual. The American Declaration of Independence* of 1776— the document in which 13 of Britain's North American colonies declared themselves independent of the British Empire—stressed the freedom and equality of all men.

Yet American slave traders and slave owners treated slaves not as individuals, but as mere property to be purchased, traded, and sold. This contradiction came from some of America's founding fathers: while progressive in some ways, they were also slave owners.

> ❝ A modern-minded reformer living in the 1770s might sum up the prospects for general emancipation … In the absence of full-scale insurrection or civil war, there will be little likelihood of persuading governments to take positive steps towards emancipation in regions dominated by the plantation system and dependent on slave labor. Even where slavery is of marginal economic importance, it will be sheltered by a concern for the rights and security of private property. An age of revolution may have begun, but revolutionary assemblies will generally be in the hands of merchants or landed interests imbued with a commercial spirit. ❞
>
> David Brion Davis, *The Problem of Slavery in the Age of Revolution, 1770–1823*

The second key theme concerns the different ways in which antislavery and abolition developed in America and Britain. America boasted one of the first active antislavery societies, the Pennsylvania Abolition Society,* founded by the Quakers* in 1775—yet the antislavery movement seemed to flounder in that country during this period, while it made great strides in Britain.

Davis does not apply his explanation for the rise of the British antislavery movement to the United States. According to him, these "abolition movements emerged in wholly different contexts."[1] In the newly independent United States, the value of liberty was exalted. This could not have been more different to Britain, where the political and social elite were hostile to social change, an attitude that had been reinforced by the American Revolution.*

The ideas of Irish statesman Edmund Burke* influenced the British outlook. Burke argued that society is an unbreakable pact between generations that is sanctioned under law. He opposed tumultuous revolutionary change, and supported the British Crown and hereditary succession.

There had been a revolution in Britain in 1688,* which abolished the absolute power of the king and replaced it with a constitutional monarchy, or a system in which Parliament limits the power of the Crown. Burke argued that this change was revolutionary enough: anything further, comparable to the French Revolution,* would be vulgar and excessive.

The American concept of liberty was influenced by the ideas of the English-American political thinker Thomas Paine;* contrary to Burke, Paine argued that under conditions of oppression such as taxation without representation, the people have the right to revolt and institute democratic rule. Paine's pamphlet *Common Sense* (1776) contrasted the new and progressive with the old and traditional.

Exploring the Ideas

Davis argues that Americans of this era had a particular concept of liberty linked to ownership of property.

Owning property was thought to imply social responsibility. Those without property were distrusted as individuals who had no stake in the new society. Slaves possessed no property. Instead, they were seen to *be* property. Paradoxically, therefore, owning a slave suggested social responsibility. Davis argued that the American "rhetoric of freedom was functionally related to the existence … of Negro slavery."[2]

One implication of this argument is that it was not race that shaped hostile white attitudes towards blacks in this period but the condition of slavery itself. As slaves had no property, they had no stake in society. And therefore they were not to be trusted.

Davis also looks at the relationship between slavery, antislavery, and abolition in the light of the rise of capitalism. The American historian Edmund S. Morgan* had argued that Americans "bought their independence with slave labor."[3] As an example, he referenced tobacco, one of the most valuable American commodities and produced through slave labor. Using this insight, Davis suggests that slavery was of fundamental importance to the national economy[4] at a time when Americans were fighting both for independence and to build their country.

Overlooked

The critical response to Davis's work has focused almost entirely on the relationship he describes between antislavery and class interests. As a result, several aspects of the text, relating mainly to the United States, have not been fully explored.

These aspects include the argument about the central role of slavery in America following the country's independence from Britain in 1776. Davis highlights the paradox* of a society that prized liberty yet relied on slavery. He shows how the American concept of liberty at that time was based on social responsibility and property ownership.

Related to this argument is Davis's discussion—one that has been neglected—about the importance of the Bible in the American debate over slavery. Davis notes that "whether the Bible was 'for' or 'against' slavery was a hotly contested issue" in the United States.[5] For nonconformist* Christian groups (those Christians who did not subscribe to orthodox ritual and belief), the Bible was at the heart of their religious beliefs. Advocates of the practice of slavery claimed that it was sanctioned by God, because the Bible contained rules relating to slavery. The core of their argument was that if slavery is referenced in the Bible, then saying that slavery is wrong undermines the divine nature of the Bible.

Antislavery advocates had to counter this. They needed to show both that slavery was wrong and that abolishing it would not undermine the Bible.

Davis notes in a later work that although historians have paid little attention to the place of the Bible in abolitionism, it was "an absolutely

central issue for American abolitionists and proslavery theorists."[6]
Davis's insight highlights the importance of engaging with the ideas of
eighteenth-century abolitionists on their own terms.

NOTES

1   David Brion Davis, "Reflections on Abolitionism and Ideological Hegemony,"
    The American Historical Review 92, no. 4 (October 1987): 798.

2   David Brion Davis, *The Problem of Slavery in the Age of Revolution, 1770–
    1823* (Ithaca: Cornell University Press, 1975), 262.

3   Quoted in Davis, *Age of Revolution*, 285.

4   Davis, *Age of Revolution*, 256.

5   Davis, *Age of Revolution*, 523.

6   David Brion Davis, "Looking at Slavery from Broader Perspectives," *The
    American Historical Review* 105, no. 4 (April 2000): 457.

MODULE 7
ACHIEVEMENT

KEY POINTS

- Davis helped to change the way the Americans and the British saw the past.

- He showed that slavery played a central role in America's battle for independence and its ability to establish itself as a new nation.

- The main limitation of Davis's work is that it covers slavery only in America, Britain, and, to a lesser extent, France. This, however, creates opportunities for further scholarship.

Assessing the Argument

In his highly influential book *Slavery in the Age of Revolution, 1770–1823* (1975), David Brion Davis addresses what happens when moral concerns clash with practical needs. The late eighteenth century saw the Industrial Revolution* developing in Britain as its former American territories, the so-called Thirteen Colonies,* were transforming themselves into a new republic: the United States of America.

This great period of economic growth meant there was a need for intensive slave labor.

Focusing on the period between 1770 and 1823, Davis asks why the social and political elite started to call into question the practice of slavery. Why was it that slavery had come to be called an intolerable practice when it provided such great economic benefits and reinforced the social structure?

By 1810 the United States and Britain had outlawed the slave trade; in 1838, Britain freed West Indian slaves.

66 Davis's study is an excellent examination of one of the key moral problems that has haunted our history. By viewing slavery in terms of the actual arguments, political struggles, economic conditions, and legal developments, one is brought to realize that there was far more at issue than the logic of the situation. **99**

Richard H. Popkin, "Review of *The Problem of Slavery in the Age of Revolution*"

Davis shows that there had been tension between oppression and the desire for humanity since biblical times. That tension was increased by the whirlwind of change brought about by the Industrial Revolution. Davis goes on to argue that British elites supported antislavery because it was practical for them to do so. At a time when many social reformers were questioning the practices of the Industrial Revolution, antislavery provided a distraction. Supporting calls for abolition allowed the ruling classes to appear progressive and responsive to social demands, and in doing so, reinforced their legitimacy.

Abolition was, therefore, both an ideological and an economic process. As Davis explains, it "opened new sources of moral prestige for the dominant social class, helped define a participatory role for middle-class activism, and looked forward to the universal goal of compliant, loyal, and self-disciplined workers."[1]

Achievement in Context

Since the 1950s, through the efforts of Davis and other historians, our understanding of the American and British past has changed radically.

Today, it is understood more widely that slavery was an integral part of the history of these nations. Historians have raised important questions about the origins of racial inequality and the way this evolved. The work of the American historian Kenneth Stampp* in his book *The Peculiar Institution* (1956) was groundbreaking in this regard.

In it, Stampp challenged the prevailing notion of black inferiority and offered new insights into America's oppressive past. This had previously been largely ignored. Scholars who came before Stampp, such as the American historian Ulrich Phillips,* had portrayed slavery as a system designed to uplift and protect African Americans; however, Stampp, inspired by the emerging civil rights movement* in America— the black struggle against racist discrimination in the 1950s and 1960s— presented vivid archival research to turn this thesis on its head.

Davis wanted to move beyond simply changing assumptions about race and human equality. He wanted his readers to understand the centrality of slavery in American history. He showed how slavery related to the development of capitalism,* particularly highlighting slaveholding presidents and how America's success was built on cotton and other labor-intensive crops. He contrasted these developments with what was happening in the British and French colonies.

Limitations

The work of David Brion Davis is widely recognized as having made an immense contribution to our understanding both of slavery and antislavery and, more broadly, of American and British history.

It is, however, acknowledged that the main limitation of *Slavery in the Age of Revolution* was Davis's narrow focus on the United States, Britain, and France. Many other nations, including Spain and Portugal, depended on slavery as they industrialized. The experiences of these countries offer parallels with and differences to the countries Davis studied. Davis himself explains that he had hoped to include more case studies, but came to realize that this was not feasible. As he acknowledges in the book, he decided to focus in depth on America and Britain rather than offer more superficial coverage of a greater number of countries.

Nevertheless, his extensive archival research and meticulously detailed work provides a foundation on which other scholars can build. As well as producing comparative findings on slavery and antislavery, future scholars could also link the analysis of slavery to broader international developments. These could include the anti-colonial struggles in Africa and Asia and the structural discrimination faced by postcolonial immigrants in European countries such as Britain, France, Holland, and Belgium.

NOTES

1   David Brion Davis, *The Problem of Slavery in the Age of Revolution, 1770–1823* (Ithaca: Cornell University Press, 1975), 385.

MODULE 8
PLACE IN THE AUTHOR'S WORK

KEY POINTS

- All of Davis's work focuses on slavery, antislavery, and abolition.*

- *The Problem of Slavery in the Age of Revolution* is the second of three books in the author's influential trilogy.

- Davis is widely recognized as an eminent historian who has greatly enhanced our knowledge of the history of slavery and emancipation.

Positioning

The Problem of Slavery in the Age of Revolution, 1770–1823 is one of the best-known and most influential works of the accomplished historian David Brion Davis. The book, the second in a trilogy, firmly established Davis as one of the leading historians of slavery and abolitionism.

The first volume in the trilogy was *The Problem of Slavery in Western Culture* (1966), a wide-ranging survey of the concept of slavery in the Western world over the last two thousand years of its history. The *Age of Revolution* begins with a summary of the central argument of *The Problem of Slavery in Western Culture*.[1] Davis spent years working on the final book in the trilogy, *The Problem of Slavery in the Age of Emancipation*. This was finally published in 2014, 30 years after the publication of what Davis called a "pilot study" for the book—his 1984 work *Slavery and Human Progress*.[2]

In *The Problem of Slavery in the Age of Emancipation*, Davis portrays the freeing of slaves as the greatest moral accomplishment in human history. This final book explores the psychology and practice of slavery, its dehumanizing effects, and the unrecognized but important role

❝ Over the past half century, Davis has come to be recognized not only as the leading authority on slavery in the Euro–Atlantic world, but also for his profound engagement with slavery's moral challenges. His sweep of study has been enormous, his command of international literatures unparalleled, his respect for other scholars exemplary, his arguments painstakingly rendered. ❞

Steven Hahn,* "The Emancipationist History"

played by freed slaves in bringing about abolition. It seeks to portray the horror of slavery and to acknowledge humanity's advances.

Integration

Davis's renowned trilogy sits within the author's wider body of work about slavery and abolitionism. Prior to the *Age of Revolution*, Davis had written *The Slave Power Conspiracy and Paranoid Style* (1969),[3] a work about conspiracy theories put forward by both advocates and opponents of slavery in the United States. Over time Davis has come to regard the idealistic motives of British and American abolitionists more sympathetically. His work has, however, continued to focus on the ideological framework of slavery and antislavery and on how ideas translate into social practices and political movements.

His other important works include *Challenging the Boundaries of Slavery* (2003),[4] a major text on slavery in the context of American history, and a wide-ranging history of the Atlantic slave trade* titled *Inhuman Bondage* (2006).[5]

Challenging the Boundaries of Slavery explores the links between the ancient world and the Age of Exploration* (the period roughly between 1400 and 1600 when the European naval powers, with ideas of commerce and land in mind, sent ships around the globe). It highlights the expansion of capitalism* and the rise in demand for sugar, tobacco, and spices.

Davis points out how the industrialization of America required the forced labor of millions of African slaves. He then shows how the American Revolution* excluded black slaves from the nation's doctrine of liberty and equality. Finally, he looks at how conflict emerged in American society over the expansion and legitimacy of slavery. In this book, as in his other works, Davis combines the reality of human tragedy with some degree of optimism about moral advancement.

In *Inhuman Bondage*, which won the Pulitzer Prize in 1967, Davis again explores the practice of slavery in the American South. He looks at cotton as a product of intense forced labor, the dehumanization of slaves by slave owners, and the emergence of an African American culture and struggle. By showing how America built its economic success on slavery, he reveals the dark side of the American dream.

Significance

Davis's work has proved enormously influential. It's widely seen as having provided the foundation for the great increase of academic interest in slavery and abolitionism.

As the American historian Joseph C. Miller* remarked in a recent retrospective on Davis's *Western Culture* and *Age of Revolution*, the work of Davis "will remain the starting point for a vast range of ongoing research and reflection."[6] This interest in Davis's ideas is likely to grow in the future thanks to the ongoing work of the Gilder Lehrman Center for Slavery, Abolition, and Resistance at Yale University. The Center was founded by Davis and now holds a lecture series in his honor. It also organizes a major annual international conference on slavery and antislavery, and aims to advance scholarly research into these issues and to bridge the gap between academia and public knowledge. It does this through collaboration with high schools, museums, parks, historical societies, and other institutions.

Davis has also become a public intellectual in the United States, well known to the general public and enthusiastic about communicating his ideas. He writes regularly for *The New York Review of Books* and has published articles explaining his insights into American history in the daily national newspaper *The New York Times*.

NOTES

1 David Brion Davis, *The Problem of Slavery in Western Culture* (Ithaca: Cornell University Press, 1966), 39–49.

2 David Brion Davis, *Slavery and Human Progress* (New York: Oxford University Press, 1984), XIX.

3 David Brion Davis, *The Slave Power Conspiracy and the Paranoid Style* (Baton Rouge: Louisiana State University Press, 1969).

4 David Brion Davis, *Challenging the Boundaries of Slavery* (Cambridge, MA: Harvard University Press, 2003).

5 David Brion Davis, *Inhuman Bondage: The Rise and Fall of Slavery in the New World* (Oxford: Oxford University Press, 2006).

6 Joseph C. Miller, *The Problem of Slavery as History* (New Haven: Yale University Press, 2012), 3.

SECTION 3
IMPACT

MODULE 9
THE FIRST RESPONSES

KEY POINTS

- Scholars have criticized Davis's depiction of hegemony* (roughly, dominance) in the British antislavery movement.

- While defending his ideas, Davis has noted that the debate has helped him to refine and fortify his argument.

- The American historian Joseph C. Miller argues that Davis's presentation of slavery as a centuries-long "institution" is wrong, as slavery took such different forms in different times and different places.

Criticism

In his book *The Problem of Slavery in the Age of Revolution, 1770–1823*, David Brion Davis talks about hegemony. By this he means a cross-class alliance that allows a small ruling class to assume the ideological and moral leadership of a society.

Davis argued that although antislavery thought emerged from the thinking of secular philosophers of the Enlightenment* (an intellectual movement of seventeenth- and eighteenth-century Europe towards rational ideas, laws, and practices) and from that of the nonconformist Christian movement known as the Quakers,* their ideas served the interests of the emerging capitalist* class. As a result, antislavery thought helped to establish the hegemony of this capitalist class and to legitimize wage labor* (the practice of working long hours—as many as 16 to 18 hours a day—in exchange for very low pay).

Different scholars have criticized this representation of hegemony. The American historian Seymour Drescher argues that

❝ [The Italian political philosopher] Antonio Gramsci*
defined 'hegemony,' in the words of his biographer, as
'the predominance, obtained by consent rather than
force, of one class or group over other classes'; or more
precisely, 'the "spontaneous" loyalty that any dominant
social group obtains from the masses by virtue of
its social and intellectual prestige and its supposedly
superior function in the world of production.' The
paramount question, which subsumes the others, is how
antislavery reinforced or legitimized such hegemony. ❞

David Brion Davis, *The Problem of Slavery in the Age of Revolution,*
1770–1823

Davis sees antislavery as a "screening device" that acted to deflect
concern over domestic problems. In fact, Drescher argues, the
antislavery movement was generated from below. It then fed into a
host of other radical causes in the nineteenth century.[1]

Another American historian, Thomas Haskell,* argues that
Davis's account is incoherent. Davis claims that antislavery advocates
were genuine in their stated principles and did not "intend" to
strengthen class hegemony. Haskell explicitly states that this is not a
valid line of argument: "To say a person is moved by class interest is
to say that he *intends* to further the interests of his class, or it is to say
nothing at all."[2]

Davis's concept of self-deception—where people convince
themselves the consequences of their actions will be different from
what they are—is very difficult to prove. This is particularly true
when reconstructing historical acts, as we surely cannot claim with
any degree of certainty to understand the psychological motives
behind them.

Responses

The critical response to *The Problem of Slavery in the Age of Revolution* had little impact on Davis's views. He claimed that many of his critics, particularly the American historian Thomas Haskell, had misinterpreted his argument. He also said that they were focusing on only a small fraction of the book.[3]

Davis published a paper in the journal *The American History Review* in 1987. Entitled "Reflections on Abolitionism and Ideological Hegemony," it stresses the distinction between the sources of antislavery thought and the conditions that enabled it to become accepted by political and economic elites. He also defends his use of the concepts of hegemony and self-deception.* For Davis, these concepts explain how British antislavery campaigners could believe they were conducting a campaign to benefit all of humanity, when they were actually strengthening the interests of a particular class.

In support of this position, Davis claims that the objections raised by the American historian Seymour Drescher—who argued that antislavery was a mass movement, not a means of diverting criticism from domestic causes—actually support his argument that the antislavery movement was hegemonic (that is, that it was a movement that belonged, so to speak, to the dominant social and political powers). The mass of the population, according to Davis, rallied behind a cause endorsed by the political elite.

Furthermore, Davis argued, even if antislavery was a mass movement in Britain, ordinary members of this movement "could not escape the fact that the governing classes succeeded in appropriating the cause and defining the terms of the debate."[4]

Davis notes that the debate provoked by *Age of Revolution* has helped him refine and clarify his argument in two ways:

- The antislavery movement was not necessarily founded as a justification for wage labor—although this was, nevertheless, the case in Britain.
- Those who were interested in promoting the status of wage labor included industrial capitalists* and "various aspiring groups, including skilled workers, who lived in a society undergoing industrialization."[5]

Conflict and Consensus

The Problem of Slavery in the Age of Revolution remains a pivotal text for students of slavery and abolitionism; a comprehensive account of the origins of the antislavery movement, it is the major reference point for anyone working on the topic.

Historians retain a high opinion of this book and of Davis's wider work. His argument that slavery occupies a central place in American history has now become a commonplace observation. This was not the case when his work was first published.

Davis's field of study now has a much wider chronological and geographical focus than just Britain and America. The experiences of other nations such as the Netherlands, Spain, and Latin America, are seen as relevant for understanding slavery and antislavery, as is slavery during later historical periods, such as that in World War II.* This means that more recent criticism of Davis's book and its predecessor, *The Problem of Slavery in Western Culture*,[6] has looked at how Davis's specific focus on the Atlantic slave trade* influenced his conception of slavery.

The American historian Seymour Drescher argues that the perception of a slave as a chattel,* a piece of moveable private property, is one that only applies to Atlantic slavery.[7] More recently, the American historian Joseph C. Miller* has argued that slavery should not be seen as an "institution" at all, since it was very different in different times and places.

This raises a serious problem for Davis's argument that the centuries-long practice of slaving was interrupted by the rise of the antislavery movement.[8]

NOTES

1   Seymour Drescher, "Cart Whip and Billy Roller: Antislavery and Reform Symbolism in Industrializing Britain," *Journal of Social History* 15, no. 1 (Autumn 1981): 4, 8–9.

2   Thomas Haskell, "Capitalism and the Origins of the Humanitarian Sensibility, Part 1," *The American Historical Review* 90, no. 2 (April 1985): 347.

3   David Brion Davis, "Reflections on Abolitionism and Ideological Hegemony," *The American Historical Review* 92 (October 1987) 4: 798.

4   Davis, "Reflections on Abolitionism," 808.

5   David Brion Davis, "The Perils of Doing History by Ahistorical Abstraction," in *The Antislavery Debate: Capitalism and Abolitionism as a Problem in Historical Interpretation*, ed. Thomas Bender (Berkley: University of California Press, 1992), 293.

6   David Brion Davis, *The Problem of Slavery in Western Culture* (Ithaca: Cornell University Press, 1966).

7   Seymour Drescher, *Abolition: A History of Slavery and Antislavery* (Cambridge: Cambridge University Press, 2009), 5.

8   Joseph C. Miller, *The Problem of Slavery as History* (New Haven: Yale University Press, 2012), 12.

MODULE 10
THE EVOLVING DEBATE

KEY POINTS

- Today, scholars are expanding on Davis's approach by relating slavery, antislavery, and abolition* to broader international developments.

- Although the author has greatly influenced other scholars, no specific school of thought has developed around him.

- Recent research has looked at the role played by the free black population of the American North in bringing about abolition.

Uses and Problems

David Brion Davis's book *The Problem of Slavery in the Age of Revolution, 1770–1823* sparked great academic interest in slavery and antislavery. Reflecting on the influence of Davis's works in 2012, the American historian Joseph C. Miller* stressed that they "will remain the starting point for a vast range of ongoing research and reflection yet to come."[1] Even historians who disagreed with Davis's argument about the development of the antislavery movement broadly accepted that there was a link between the emergence of antislavery ideas and the rise of capitalism.

Historians now tend to take a wider view, however, of the conditions and historical experiences that shaped antislavery movements and ended the Atlantic slave trade.* For example, the British historian Will Pettigrew* argues in his book *Freedom's Debt* (2003) that some progressive representatives of the Royal African Company—a state-sponsored corporation that spearheaded Britain's slave trade—expressed concern regarding the brutality of slavery. This,

❝ Davis is fully aware of the moral ambiguities involved in the crusade against slavery, the process of abolition and the long afterlife of racism. Nonetheless, in a rebuke to those historians today who belittle the entire project of emancipation, he insists that the abolition of slavery in the Western Hemisphere was one of the profoundest achievements in human history. **❞**

Eric Foner, "Slavery in the Modern World"

Pettigrew argues, provided inspiration for the antislavery movement of the eighteenth century. This view gives greater primacy to moral consciousness than to economics.[2]

In 2006, a collection of essays called *Prophets of Protest* was published. The essays were written by leading scholars who argued that abolition was the result of a diverse social movement that emerged after the American Revolution.* As the free black population began to grow in the American North, its members came to realize that the white population would not ensure that the Revolution's rhetoric of equality would become a reality. So they took on the challenge of producing change themselves. Through a combination of almost every means possible, from newspapers and fiction to photography, parades and music, they challenged injustice and eventually created sufficient pressure for abolition to take place.[3]

Schools of Thought

It is difficult to separate the influence of *The Problem of Slavery in the Age of Revolution* from Davis's influence more generally. This difficulty is compounded by the fact that he has continued to produce highly regarded work in the decades since *Age of Revolution* was published. Although no academic school has formed around Davis's text, his work has had an enormous impact on the discipline.

The amount of academic work now being produced in this field is staggering, and much of it uses Davis's texts as central reference points. The University of Virginia maintains a bibliography of academic works on slavery; by the mid-2000s, over 1,200 titles were being added to this compilation every year.[4] Recent scholarship emphasizes the international context of abolitionism. However, the British antislavery movement—one of the primary focuses of *Age of Revolution* and the earliest and most successful movement—remains a key area of study.

Subsequent research into this area of British history has been led by Davis's careful focus on the domestic context of antislavery. The British historian John Oldfield,* for instance, has built on Davis's work on the origins of British antislavery and the reasons behind its mass appeal. He has looked at how this movement was organized on the ground, and at how it became a precursor to the growth of mass politics in Britain in the nineteenth century.

In Current Scholarship

Although *The Problem of Slavery in the Age of Revolution* remains a key work, the influence of Davis himself is wider than the influence of this one text.

In his long and distinguished career as an academic, Davis taught a large number of students, many of whom have gone on to become academic historians. More widely, virtually all historians working on the history of slavery and antislavery, at least in the Anglo-American world, can be seen to be building on Davis's work.

Davis can take much of the credit for helping to ignite academic interest in slavery and the interplay between values, morality, and social experience. Many of his former students have gone on to explore how American society has confronted moral problems in different historical periods. In 1998 the collection of essays *Moral Problems in American Life* was published. Each of the 15 contributors notes that they "owe a profound debt to our teacher and mentor, David Brion Davis." They acknowledge that his work provided the model for theirs.[5]

Other academics influenced by Davis's work are grouped around the Gilder Lehrman Center for Slavery, Abolition, and Resistance at Yale University. Founded by Davis in 1998, it has become one of preeminent centers for slavery and antislavery studies in the world.

NOTES

1   See Joseph C. Miller, *The Problem of Slavery as History* (New Haven: Yale University Press, 2012), 3.

2   William Pettigrew, *Freedom's Debt: The Royal African Company and the Politics of the African Slave Trade, 1672–1752* (Chapel Hill: University of North Carolina Press, 2013), 214.

3   Timothy Patrick McCarthy and John Stauffer, eds, *Prophets of Protest: Reconsidering the History of American Abolitionism* (New York: The New Press, 2006).

4   For the latest additions to the bibliography, see Thomas Thurston, "Slavery Annual Bibliographical Supplement (2012)," *Slavery & Abolition* 34, no. 4 (2013): 693–781.

5   Karen Halttunen and Lewis W. Perry, *Moral Problems in American Life: New Perspectives in Cultural History* (Ithaca: Cornell University Press, 1998), 10.

MODULE 11
IMPACT AND INFLUENCE TODAY

KEY POINTS

- Davis's work is most relevant to the fields of history and sociology and the sub-field of African American studies.

- Davis's insight that slavery was a central part of American history is widely accepted today.

- Davis's link between moral thought and social change continues to be challenged by other scholars.

Position

The impact of David Brion Davis's book *The Problem of Slavery in the Age of Revolution, 1770–1823* has been limited to the fields of history and sociology and the sub-field of African American studies. Outside these disciplines, the text has not attracted attention. Davis wrote about the relationship between antislavery and the law, for example, but no legal scholars have expanded on this. Davis himself was not seeking to make a general contribution to a wider audience; his aim was to contribute to a particular historical debate and to fill the gap in American historiography* (that is, in written works of American history) around slavery, antislavery, and abolition.

Some historians, many of them Davis's former students, have been inspired by his conception of antislavery as "a profound transformation in moral perception." They have gone on to examine how American society has confronted moral problems at other points in the past.[1] Other historians have used his argument about how slavery coexisted with (and contradicted) the rhetoric* of liberty and equality during the American Revolution.* They have used this as a starting point from which to explore American ideas about freedom in greater depth.[2] The

❝ David Brion Davis has been the preeminent historian of ideas about slavery in the Western world since the early modern period. ... Davis, a leading practitioner of intellectual and cultural history, has now gone far beyond the history of ideas and attempted to study New World slavery in all its ramifications, social, economic, and political, as well as intellectual and cultural. ... He convincingly demonstrates that slavery was central to the history of the New World. ❞

George Fredrickson, "They'll Take Their Stand"

bulk of the work inspired by *Age of Revolution* and Davis's wider corpus, though, continues to relate to the history of slavery and antislavery.

Interaction

Although *The Problem of Slavery in the Age of Revolution* is central to the modern study of slavery and antislavery, the book focuses on the Anglo-American experience. By the standards of current historiography this is a narrow approach; research now takes a broader view of slavery, looking further afield both geographically and chronologically.

Other experiences of slavery elsewhere in the world are now seen as relevant to understanding the form slavery took during the Atlantic slave trade.* These include experiences of slavery in Spain's American colonies (including those that are now part of the modern-day United States), earlier Dutch involvement in the slave trade, and slavery in what is often called the "Islamic world." Some historians also believe that slavery during later historical periods, such as that in World War II,* sheds light on the experience of slavery and antislavery during the nineteenth century.

When the book was first published in 1975 it presented a new challenge to conventional thinking about slavery. In the book Davis stresses the central position of slavery in the history of the United States—an argument generally accepted today.

One of Davis's other ideas, however, still presents a challenge to mainstream thought about the abolition of slavery. While the conventional version of abolition emphasizes the idealism of antislavery campaigners, which is regarded as the driving force behind the end of slavery, Davis draws attention to a different force behind abolition. He argues that the mass antislavery movement—which appeared after centuries of the practice being accepted and justified— emerged almost simultaneously with the rise of a new economic system: capitalism.*

This link between capitalism and abolition is one of the book's central ideas.

The Continuing Debate

Interest in the subjects of slavery and antislavery has increased enormously since the publication of *The Problem of Slavery in the Age of Revolution* in 1975. Today, Davis's text is a key point of reference in the scholarly debate over slavery and antislavery rather than comprising a set of arguments being actively responded to by academics. Davis has made minor revisions to his arguments, and these have elicited responses from his critics—a process that has led to further advances in the way we understand the field.

Although slavery remains an emotive issue for many people, criticism of Davis's work has been professional rather than motivated by personal hostility or ideological disagreement. Even Davis's most persistent critics have praised his work as a major contribution to the field. For example, the American historian Thomas Haskell,* responding to Davis's rejection of his criticisms of *The Problem of Slavery in the Age of Revolution*, prefaces his further criticism by saying:

"Davis's volumes on slavery constitute one of the towering achievements of historical scholarship in our generation."[3]

The debate between the two has sometimes bordered on being ill tempered; Davis has accused Haskell several times of misquoting him,[4] which Haskell denies. However, the debate is a professional and important one. The discussion with Haskell has been generated by the significant implications of Davis's argument about the link between moral thought and social change.

NOTES

1   David Brion Davis, *The Problem of Slavery in the Age of Revolution, 1770–1823* (Ithaca: Cornell University Press, 1975),11; Karen Halttunen and Lewis W. Perry, *Moral Problems in American Life: New Perspectives in Cultural History* (Ithaca: Cornell University Press, 1998).

2   See, for instance, Eric Foner, "The Meaning of Freedom in the Age of Emancipation," *The Journal of American History* 81, no. 2 (1994): 435–60.

3   Thomas Haskell, "Convention and Hegemonic Interest in the Debate over Antislavery: a Reply to Davis and Ashworth," *The American Historical Review* 92, no. 3 (1992): 830.

4   David Brion Davis, "Reflections on Abolitionism and Ideological Hegemony," *The American Historical Review* 92, no. 4 (October 1987): 798.

MODULE 12
WHERE NEXT?

KEY POINTS

- Since publishing *The Problem of Slavery in the Age of Revolution*, David Brion Davis has become more sympathetic to the idea that the abolitionists had moral convictions.

- Scholars have proved that Britain's slave colonies were not in economic decline when slavery was abolished.

- Davis's sequel to *The Problem of Slavery in the Age of Revolution* explores slavery in other parts of the world.

Potential

David Brion Davis's book *The Problem of Slavery in the Age of Revolution, 1770–1823*, along with his other works, is likely to remain important for historians. In the 1970s and 1980s the work generated a major debate about the link between the rise of capitalism* and the emergence of antislavery.

Today, this issue has become less central to the study of slavery. Where it is discussed, the emphasis is now on a broader investigation of the political nature of the economy rather than simply being a narrow look at the industrial class struggle.

Tellingly, Davis himself has moved away from this argument in its earlier form. He now has a wider focus, looking at the link between a broadly supported desire to dignify labor and receptivity to antislavery ideas.[2] Davis also takes a more sympathetic view of the abolitionists'* campaign. He now regards it as firm evidence of moral convictions overcoming material interest.[3]

❝ We must face the ultimate contradiction that our free and democratic society was made possible by massive slave labor.[1] **❞**

David Brion Davis, *The Rise and Fall of Slavery in the New World*

This re-emphasis on the importance of ideology may increase the relevance of the book to future studies of antislavery. Since the publication of *The Problem of Slavery in the Age of Revolution* scholars have—convincingly—disproved the thesis that Britain's slave colonies were in decline when the British abolished slavery.[4] This strongly suggests, then, that it was ideological or political change that was behind the decision to abolish slavery rather than economic considerations alone. This focus on ideology reflects Davis's ideas about the link between moral thought and social change.

Future Directions

It is the job of scholars to debunk prevailing myths and detail lost narratives, revealing all the dark tales in a nation's history. For a long time, the reality of slavery was obscured in the United States and Britain. To some extent, this is still the case. There is plenty of room for further scholarship on the subject.

Davis's work plays a key role in exposing these realities. His ideas built on, and complemented, the work of other historians. Now further comparative analyses are being carried out to account for the ways in which slavery and antislavery have developed in other contexts.

Davis himself has highlighted how much work is still to be done. *Slavery in the Age of Emancipation*, the final book in his critically acclaimed trilogy, was published in 2014. Davis said that when he started researching this work he was struck by how little scholars had paid attention to the Haitian Revolution*—the slave revolt in the

French colony of Saint-Domingue that lasted from 1791 to 1804, leading to the elimination of slavery in the colony and the founding of the Republic of Haiti.

Davis had touched upon some aspects of this revolution in his earlier works, but he had not studied it in significant detail. In *Slavery in the Age of Emancipation* he does focus on Haiti, relating the events there to progressive action in Britain and elsewhere. During the course of his analysis, he examines how white populations dehumanized the black population. When this process of dehumanization was condemned, it brought hope that black populations elsewhere in the world could be emancipated. This final volume of Davis's trilogy is a good example of the way in which scholars can build on previous work to improve our understanding of history.

Summary

Davis's most significant and influential idea in *The Problem of Slavery in the Age of Revolution* is that the British opposition to slavery must be considered alongside the vast economic changes that were occurring at that time.

While he stresses the religious and philosophical origins of antislavery ideas, Davis argues that an unintended consequence of the antislavery movement was that it helped to legitimize the emerging capitalist work structure. But it was this unforeseen link that motivated the British elite to argue for abolition, as it supported class interests.

Davis is not a Marxist* historian. That is, he does not conduct his analysis of historical events through the prism of economic and class interests first proposed by the economist and political theorist Karl Marx. Rather, Davis defines class as "something far more complex than a group united or governed by purely economic interest."[5]

He also argues that "class interest" can work in subtle ways. Antislavery campaigners and the British elite did not have a direct financial stake in the ending of slavery. They benefited from the campaign in other ways. Borrowing the Italian Marxist thinker Antonio Gramsci's* concept of "hegemony,"* Davis argues that antislavery bolstered the ruling class by legitimizing their rule. It created a cross-class alliance that helped them to rule by consent, rather than by force.[6]

Davis emphasizes that although many prominent abolitionists came to benefit from the capitalist system, this was not what motivated them to campaign for abolition. They were genuine and sincere opponents of slavery. Davis argues that the advancing of class interests was not always a product of conscious choice. He uses the concept of the American social scientist Peter Berger,* who said that people, in this instance antislavery advocates, are capable of deceiving themselves about their true needs and interests.

As the Quakers* moved increasingly into industry, they became more conscious of the distinction between free and slave labor. This came to be reflected in their antislavery writing. With reference to this, Davis uses the concept of self-deception to explain the discrepancy between the humanitarian concerns of antislavery advocates and their lack of concern about exploitation in British industry.

NOTES

1 David Brion Davis, *Inhuman Bondage: The Rise and Fall of Slavery in the New World* (Oxford: Oxford University Press, 2006), 6.

2 Davis, *Inhuman Bondage*, 248.

3 Davis, *Inhuman Bondage*, 238, 249.

4 For an overview of these, see Seymour Drescher, *From Slavery to Freedom: Comparative Studies in the Rise and Fall of Atlantic Slavery* (London: Macmillan, 1999).

5 David Brion Davis, *The Problem of Slavery in the Age of Revolution, 1770–1823* (Ithaca: Cornell University Press, 1975), 182.

6 Davis, *Age of Revolution*, 348–9.

GLOSSARY

GLOSSARY OF TERMS

Abolitionism: a movement to end slavery that began in Britain in the late eighteenth century and gained increasing popularity in the United States in the early nineteenth century.

Age of Exploration: a period from roughly 1400 to 1600 in which Europeans explored the rest of the world for goods, raw materials, and land.

Age of Revolution: a term David Brion Davis uses to refer to the period between 1770 and 1823 when progressives (that is, people invested in social reform) in Britain and America more actively condemned slavery.

American Civil War (1861–65): a war fought in the United States when seven (rising to 13) Southern states formed the Confederate States and declared their independence after the election of President Abraham Lincoln, who led the Unionist states in the North.

Capitalism (or industrial capitalism): an economic system that emphasizes the private ownership of the means of production. "The means of production" refers to those things—such as land, natural resources, and technology—that are necessary for the production of goods.

Chattel: this refers to a piece of movable private property.

Civil rights movement: the period in the 1950s and 1960s when black people in the United States struggled against discrimination and for greater equality.

Declaration of Independence: the document written by the American revolutionaries in 1776 declaring their intention to create a new state and listing their grievances against the British government.

Enlightenment: also known as "the Age of Reason," this was a Western intellectual movement of the seventeenth and eighteenth centuries that aimed to question tradition and religious belief while advancing knowledge of the world through scientific method.

French Revolution: this took place between 1789 and 1799. It was a period of deep political and social transformation in France; it influenced the course of Western history as a whole.

Haitian Revolution: a slave revolt in the French colony of Saint-Domingue from 1791 to 1804, which led to the elimination of slavery and the founding of the Republic of Haiti.

Hegemony: borrowing the Marxist political theorist Antonio Gramsci's* concept of hegemony, Davis argues that antislavery bolstered the dominance (or hegemony) of the ruling class by creating a cross-class alliance. This helped enable them to rule by consent, rather than by force, over other classes in society by legitimating their rule.

Historiography: the writing of history.

Idealism: the practice of envisioning something in an ideal and often unrealistic form.

Ideology: a system of ideas and ideals, particularly forming the basis of economic or political theory and policy.

Industrial Revolution: a period of rapid economic and social change that began in England in the eighteenth century and later spread to Western Europe and the United States. It was characterized by a shift from an agrarian (that is, agricultural) economy of manual labor to one dominated by machines and industry.

Laissez-faire: this is an attitude or a policy of letting things take their own course, without interfering. It is normally used in reference to the free market.

Marxism: the name ascribed to the political system advocated by the political theorist and economist Karl Marx. It emphasized an end to capitalism by taking control of the means of production from individuals and placing it in the hands of central government.

Monarchy: a form of government where supremacy lies with a single, usually hereditary, figure, such as a king or queen.

Nationalism: the ideology that advocates a nation's inherent superiority. The word is also used to indicate a political movement aimed at achieving a nation's independence.

Natural rights: these, according to the eighteenth-century political theorist Thomas Paine, are those rights to which all human beings are entitled by virtue of their existence.

Nonconformist: a person who does not conform to, or refuses to be bound by, accepted beliefs, customs, or practices.

Paradox: a person, thing, or situation that exhibits inexplicable or contradictory aspects

Pennsylvania Abolition Society: an organization formed in 1775 to offer relief to free black people unlawfully held in bondage.

Planter class: this refers to planters in the American South who owned large numbers of slaves.

Pulitzer Prize: a prestigious award for American journalism, literature, and music.

Quakers: a Christian movement founded by George Fox, an English religious leader, in about 1650. Officially known as the Religious Society of Friends, their core belief centers on "the doctrine of the Inner Light."

Reductionism: any theory or method that reduces a complex idea or system to its simpler parts or components.

Revolution of 1688: in English history, also known as the Glorious Revolution, or Bloodless Revolution. It resulted in the unseating of King James II and the ascension to the throne of his daughter Mary II, who ruled jointly with her husband William III.

Rhetoric: the use of elaborate language for a persuasive or impressive effect, but lacking in sincerity or meaningful content.

Slave trade: the transportation of black Africans to America between the sixteenth and nineteenth centuries.

Thirteen Colonies: the American territories that declared their independence from Britain in 1776.

US Constitution: a document adopted in 1787 and ratified in 1789 that acts as the supreme law of the United States of America. It considers unconstitutional any attempts by the states to nullify its laws.

Utilitarianism: this is a doctrine that argues that the correct action is one that ensures the greatest happiness for the greatest number of people.

Wage labor: this came into being during the Industrial Revolution, when people worked long hours (as many as 16 to 18 hours a day) in exchange for very low pay. Furthermore, workers were obliged to spend these wages at company stores, which in turn produced further profit.

War of Independence: a revolutionary war from 1775 to 1783 in which Great Britain's colonies in North America won political independence from the British Empire and went on to form the United States of America.

World War II (1939–45): a global war between the vast majority of world states, including all the great powers of the time.

PEOPLE MENTIONED IN THE TEXT

Roger Anstey (1927–1979) was a historian of central Africa, the Atlantic slave trade, and intellectual history. One of his best-known works is *The Atlantic Slave Trade and British Abolition, 1760–1810* (1975).

Peter Berger (b. 1929) is an American sociologist based at Boston University whose primary research focuses on the relationship between society and the individual. His most influential work is perhaps *Invitation to Sociology: A Humanistic Perspective* (1966).

Edmund Burke (1729–1797) was a British statesman and political thinker. He is considered the father of modern conservatism for his arguments in *Reflections on the Revolution in France* (1790) against political and social reform.

Seymour Drescher (b. 1934) is a professor based at the University of Pittsburgh and is one of the foremost historians of slavery. He is best known for his highly influential work *Econocide: British Slavery in the Era of Abolition* (1977).

Drew Gilpin Faust (b. 1947) is an American historian and the president of Harvard University. She is the author of several books, including *Mothers of Intervention: Women of the Slaveholding South in the American Civil War* (1996).

Eric Foner (b. 1943) is an American historian and professor of history at Columbia University. He has published several important works, including *The Fiery Trial: Abraham Lincoln and American Slavery* (2010).

George Fredrickson (1934–2008) was Edgar E. Robinson
Professor of History at Stanford University. He was an American
expert in comparative history and racism.

Antonio Gramsci (1891–1937) was an Italian Marxist theoretician
whose hugely influential ideas on hegemony offered an explanation
for how a small ruling class establishes and maintains a dominant
position in capitalist society. He remains best known for the
posthumously published *Prison Notebooks*.

Steven Hahn is Roy F. and Jeannette P. Nichols Professor in
American History at the University of Pennsylvania. He has written
several important works, including *The Roots of Southern Populism:
Yeoman Farmers and the Transformation of the Georgia Upcountry, 1850–
1890* (1983).

Thomas Haskell is Professor Emeritus at Rice University and a
historian specializing in American intellectual history. He is perhaps
best known for *The Culture of the Market: Historical Essays* (1993), a
volume he co-edited with the historian Richard F. Teichgraeber.

Karl Marx (1818–83) was a German philosopher, economist,
historian, and sociologist who is widely considered to be one of the
most influential social scientists.

Joseph Miller (b. 1940) is a professor at the University of Virginia
who has worked on African history and the Atlantic slave trade.

Gunnar Myrdal (1898–1987) was a Swedish economist and
sociologist who won the Nobel Prize for Economics in 1974. One of
his most famous works is *An American Dilemma: The Negro Problem and
Modern Democracy* (1944).

Edmund S. Morgan (1916–2013) was a noted authority on early American history and was a professor at Yale University for much of his professional life. He produced a seminal work on American history entitled *The Birth of the Republic, 1763–1789* (1956).

Napoleon Bonaparte (1769–1821) was the first emperor of France and one of the most well known military leaders in Western history.

Barack Obama (b. 1961) is the 44th president of the United States and the first African American to hold that office.

John Oldfield is a historian based at the University of Southampton whose primarily interest is the slave trade. One of his first major works was *Popular Politics and British Antislavery: The Mobilisation of Public Opinion Against the Slave Trade, 1787–1807* (1998).

Thomas Paine (1737–1809) was an influential English American political writer and propagandist. His works include *Common Sense* (1776), *Rights of Man* (1791–92), and *The Age of Reason* (1794), which, respectively, influenced the American Revolution, defended the French Revolution, and explored the place of religion in society.

William Pettigrew (1825–1906) is reader (associate professor) at the University of Kent. He is an expert on the transatlantic slave trade and the author of *Freedom's Debt* (2013).

Ulrich Phillips (1877–1934) was a historian who made immense contributions to our understanding of the social and economic history of the American South and slavery.

William Pitt (1759–1806) was the British prime minister between 1783 and 1804, and again between 1804 and 1806. He is known as Pitt the Younger, to distinguish him from his father, also called William Pitt, who was prime minister between 1766 and 1768 .

Richard H. Popkin (1923–2005), an academic philosopher and historian of the Enlightenment, he was distinguished professor at City University of New York.

Kenneth Stampp (1912–2009) was professor emeritus of history at the University of California at Berkeley. He was a renowned scholar of slavery, the American Civil War, and Reconstruction

Eric Williams (1911–81) was the first prime minister of Trinidad and Tobago as well as being a historian of the Caribbean. His book *Capitalism and Slavery* (1944) has had an enduring influence on debates about antislavery.

WORKS CITED

WORKS CITED

Anstey, Roger. *The Atlantic Slave Trade and British Abolition, 1760–1810*. London: Macmillan, 1975.

"Capitalism and Slavery, a Critique." *The Economic History Review* 21, no. 2 (August 1968): 307–20.

Bender, Thomas, ed. *The Antislavery Debate: Capitalism and Abolitionism as a Problem in Historical Interpretation*. Berkley: University of California Press, 1992.

Berger, Peter. *Invitation to Sociology: A Humanistic Perspective*. Harmondsworth: Penguin, 1966.

Davis, David Brion. "The American Dilemma." *The New York Review of Books*, July 16, 1992.

Challenging the Boundaries of Slavery. Cambridge, MA: Harvard University Press, 2003.

Inhuman Bondage: The Rise and Fall of Slavery in the New World. Oxford: Oxford University Press, 2006.

"Looking at Slavery from Broader Perspectives." *The American Historical Review* 105, no. 4 (April 2000) 4: 452–66.

The Problem of Slavery in the Age of Revolution. Ithaca: Cornell University Press, 1975.

The Problem of Slavery in Western Culture. Ithaca: Cornell University Press, 1966.

"Re-Examining the Problems of Slavery in Western Culture." *The Proceedings of the American Antiquarian Society* 1038 (October 2008): 247–66.

"Reflections on Abolitionism and Ideological Hegemony." *The American Historical Review* 92, no. 4 (October 1987): 797–812.

The Slave Power Conspiracy and the Paranoid Style. Baton Rouge: Louisiana State University Press, 1969.

Slavery and Human Progress. New York: Oxford University Press, 1984.

"World War II and Memory." *The Journal of American History* 77 (September 1990) 2: 580–7.

Drescher, Seymour. *Abolition: A History of Slavery and Antislavery*. Cambridge: Cambridge University Press, 2009.

"Cart Whip and Billy Roller: Antislavery and Reform Symbolism in Industrializing Britain." *Journal of Social History* 15, no. 1 (Autumn 1981): 3–24.

Econocide: British Slavery in the Era of Abolition. Pittsburgh: Pittsburgh University Press, 1977.

"Public Opinion and the Destruction of British Colonial Slavery." In *Slavery and British Society, 1776–1846*, edited by James Walvin, 22–48. London: Macmillan, 1982.

Foner, Eric. "The Meaning of Freedom in the Age of Emancipation." *The Journal of American History* 81, no. 2 (1994): 435–60.

Fredrickson, George. "They'll Take Their Stand." *The New York Review of Books*, May 25, 2006. Accessed May 29, 2015. http://www.nybooks.com/articles/archives/2006/may/25/theyll-take-their-stand/.

Gramsci, Antonio. *Selections from the Prison Notebooks of Antonio Gramsci.* Translated by Quintin Hoare and Geoffrey Nowell-Smith. London: Lawrence & Wishart, 1971.

Halttunen, Karen, and Lewis W. Perry, eds. *Moral Problems in American Life: New Perspectives in Cultural History.* Ithaca: Cornell University Press, 1998.

Haskell, Thomas. "Capitalism and the Origins of the Humanitarian Sensibility, Part 1." *The American Historical Review* 90, no. 2 (April 1985): 339–61.

"Capitalism and the Origins of the Humanitarian Sensibility, Part 2." *The American Historical Review* 90, no. 3 (June 1985): 547–66.

"Convention and Hegemonic Interest in the Debate over Antislavery: A Reply to Davis and Ashworth." *The American Historical Review* 92, no. 3 (1992): 829–78.

Haskell, Thomas, and Richard F. Teichgraeber, eds. *The Culture of the Market: Historical Essays.* Cambridge: Cambridge University Press, 1993.

Lecky, William E. H. *History of European Morals from Augustus to Charlemagne Vol. 1.* 3rd ed. London: Longman, Green, and Company, 1877.

Leuchtenburg, William, ed. *American Places: Encounters with History: A Celebration of Sheldon Meyer.* Oxford: Oxford University Press, 2000.

McCarthy, Timothy Patrick, and John Stauffer, eds. *Prophets of Protest: Reconsidering the History of American Abolitionism.* New York: The New Press, 2006.

Miller, Joseph C. *The Problem of Slavery as History.* New Haven: Yale University Press, 2012.

Morgan, Edmund. *The Birth of the Republic, 1763–1789*. Chicago: University of Chicago Press, 1956.

Myrdal, Gunnar. *An American Dilemma: The Negro Problem and Modern Democracy.* New York: Harper & Brothers, 1944.

Oldfield, John. *Popular Politics and British Antislavery: The Mobilisation of Public Opinion Against the Slave Trade, 1787–1807*. London: Cass, 1998.

Transatlantic Abolitionism in the Age of Revolution: An International History of Antislavery. Cambridge: Cambridge University Press, 2013.

Parry, Marc. "The Long Reach of David Brion Davis." *Chronicle of Higher Education*, February 3, 2014. Accessed May 29, 2015. http://chronicle.com/article/The-Long-Reach-of-David-Brion/144287/.

Pettigrew, William. *Freedom's Debt: The Royal African Company and the Politics of the African Slave Trade, 1672–1752*. Chapel Hill: University of North Carolina Press, 2013.

Popkin, Richard H. "The Problem of Slavery in the Age of Revolution" (review). *Journal of the History of Philosophy* 16, no. 4 (1978): 482–5.

Stampp, Kenneth. *The Peculiar Institution: Slavery in the Ante-Bellum South*. New York: Knopf, 1956.

Thurston, Thomas. "Slavery Annual Bibliographical Supplement (2012)." *Slavery & Abolition* 34, no. 4 (2013): 693–781.

Williams, Eric. *Capitalism and Slavery*. Chapel Hill: University of North Carolina Press, 1944.

Wood, Peter H. "Negotiating a Settlement in the Long War of Slavery." *Reviews in American History* 3, no. 3 (September 1975): 310–16.

Yerxa, Donald A. "On Slavery and Antislavery: An Interview with David Brion Davis." *Historically Speaking* (July–August 2007).

THE MACAT LIBRARY
BY DISCIPLINE

AFRICANA STUDIES

Chinua Achebe's *An Image of Africa: Racism in Conrad's Heart of Darkness*
W. E. B. Du Bois's *The Souls of Black Folk*
Zora Neale Huston's *Characteristics of Negro Expression*
Martin Luther King Jr's *Why We Can't Wait*
Toni Morrison's *Playing in the Dark: Whiteness in the American Literary Imagination*

ANTHROPOLOGY

Arjun Appadurai's *Modernity at Large: Cultural Dimensions of Globalisation*
Philippe Ariès's *Centuries of Childhood*
Franz Boas's *Race, Language and Culture*
Kim Chan & Renée Mauborgne's *Blue Ocean Strategy*
Jared Diamond's *Guns, Germs & Steel: the Fate of Human Societies*
Jared Diamond's *Collapse: How Societies Choose to Fail or Survive*
E. E. Evans-Pritchard's *Witchcraft, Oracles and Magic Among the Azande*
James Ferguson's *The Anti-Politics Machine*
Clifford Geertz's *The Interpretation of Cultures*
David Graeber's *Debt: the First 5000 Years*
Karen Ho's *Liquidated: An Ethnography of Wall Street*
Geert Hofstede's *Culture's Consequences: Comparing Values, Behaviors, Institutes and Organizations across Nations*
Claude Lévi-Strauss's *Structural Anthropology*
Jay Macleod's *Ain't No Makin' It: Aspirations and Attainment in a Low-Income Neighborhood*
Saba Mahmood's *The Politics of Piety: The Islamic Revival and the Feminist Subjec*t
Marcel Mauss's *The Gift*

BUSINESS

Jean Lave & Etienne Wenger's *Situated Learning*
Theodore Levitt's *Marketing Myopia*
Burton G. Malkiel's *A Random Walk Down Wall Street*
Douglas McGregor's *The Human Side of Enterprise*
Michael Porter's *Competitive Strategy: Creating and Sustaining Superior Performance*
John Kotter's *Leading Change*
C. K. Prahalad & Gary Hamel's *The Core Competence of the Corporation*

CRIMINOLOGY

Michelle Alexander's *The New Jim Crow: Mass Incarceration in the Age of Colorblindness*
Michael R. Gottfredson & Travis Hirschi's *A General Theory of Crime*
Richard Herrnstein & Charles A. Murray's *The Bell Curve: Intelligence and Class Structure in American Life*
Elizabeth Loftus's *Eyewitness Testimony*
Jay Macleod's *Ain't No Makin' It: Aspirations and Attainment in a Low-Income Neighborhood*
Philip Zimbardo's *The Lucifer Effect*

ECONOMICS

Janet Abu-Lughod's *Before European Hegemony*
Ha-Joon Chang's *Kicking Away the Ladder*
David Brion Davis's *The Problem of Slavery in the Age of Revolution*
Milton Friedman's *The Role of Monetary Policy*
Milton Friedman's *Capitalism and Freedom*
David Graeber's *Debt: the First 5000 Years*
Friedrich Hayek's *The Road to Serfdom*
Karen Ho's *Liquidated: An Ethnography of Wall Street*

The Macat Library By Discipline

John Maynard Keynes's *The General Theory of Employment, Interest and Money*
Charles P. Kindleberger's *Manias, Panics and Crashes*
Robert Lucas's *Why Doesn't Capital Flow from Rich to Poor Countries?*
Burton G. Malkiel's *A Random Walk Down Wall Street*
Thomas Robert Malthus's *An Essay on the Principle of Population*
Karl Marx's *Capital*
Thomas Piketty's *Capital in the Twenty-First Century*
Amartya Sen's *Development as Freedom*
Adam Smith's *The Wealth of Nations*
Nassim Nicholas Taleb's *The Black Swan: The Impact of the Highly Improbable*
Amos Tversky's & Daniel Kahneman's *Judgment under Uncertainty: Heuristics and Biases*
Mahbub Ul Haq's *Reflections on Human Development*
Max Weber's *The Protestant Ethic and the Spirit of Capitalism*

FEMINISM AND GENDER STUDIES

Judith Butler's *Gender Trouble*
Simone De Beauvoir's *The Second Sex*
Michel Foucault's *History of Sexuality*
Betty Friedan's *The Feminine Mystique*
Saba Mahmood's *The Politics of Piety: The Islamic Revival and the Feminist Subject*
Joan Wallach Scott's *Gender and the Politics of History*
Mary Wollstonecraft's *A Vindication of the Rights of Woman*
Virginia Woolf's *A Room of One's Own*

GEOGRAPHY

The Brundtland Report's *Our Common Future*
Rachel Carson's *Silent Spring*
Charles Darwin's *On the Origin of Species*
James Ferguson's *The Anti-Politics Machine*
Jane Jacobs's *The Death and Life of Great American Cities*
James Lovelock's *Gaia: A New Look at Life on Earth*
Amartya Sen's *Development as Freedom*
Mathis Wackernagel & William Rees's *Our Ecological Footprint*

HISTORY

Janet Abu-Lughod's *Before European Hegemony*
Benedict Anderson's *Imagined Communities*
Bernard Bailyn's *The Ideological Origins of the American Revolution*
Hanna Batatu's *The Old Social Classes And The Revolutionary Movements Of Iraq*
Christopher Browning's *Ordinary Men: Reserve Police Batallion 101 and the Final Solution in Poland*
Edmund Burke's *Reflections on the Revolution in France*
William Cronon's *Nature's Metropolis: Chicago And The Great West*
Alfred W. Crosby's *The Columbian Exchange*
Hamid Dabashi's *Iran: A People Interrupted*
David Brion Davis's *The Problem of Slavery in the Age of Revolution*
Nathalie Zemon Davis's *The Return of Martin Guerre*
Jared Diamond's *Guns, Germs & Steel: the Fate of Human Societies*
Frank Dikotter's *Mao's Great Famine*
John W Dower's *War Without Mercy: Race And Power In The Pacific War*
W. E. B. Du Bois's *The Souls of Black Folk*
Richard J. Evans's *In Defence of History*
Lucien Febvre's *The Problem of Unbelief in the 16th Century*
Sheila Fitzpatrick's *Everyday Stalinism*

Eric Foner's *Reconstruction: America's Unfinished Revolution, 1863-1877*
Michel Foucault's *Discipline and Punish*
Michel Foucault's *History of Sexuality*
Francis Fukuyama's *The End of History and the Last Man*
John Lewis Gaddis's *We Now Know: Rethinking Cold War History*
Ernest Gellner's *Nations and Nationalism*
Eugene Genovese's *Roll, Jordan, Roll: The World the Slaves Made*
Carlo Ginzburg's *The Night Battles*
Daniel Goldhagen's *Hitler's Willing Executioners*
Jack Goldstone's *Revolution and Rebellion in the Early Modern World*
Antonio Gramsci's *The Prison Notebooks*
Alexander Hamilton, John Jay & James Madison's *The Federalist Papers*
Christopher Hill's *The World Turned Upside Down*
Carole Hillenbrand's *The Crusades: Islamic Perspectives*
Thomas Hobbes's *Leviathan*
Eric Hobsbawm's *The Age Of Revolution*
John A. Hobson's *Imperialism: A Study*
Albert Hourani's *History of the Arab Peoples*
Samuel P. Huntington's *The Clash of Civilizations and the Remaking of World Order*
C. L. R. James's *The Black Jacobins*
Tony Judt's *Postwar: A History of Europe Since 1945*
Ernst Kantorowicz's *The King's Two Bodies: A Study in Medieval Political Theology*
Paul Kennedy's *The Rise and Fall of the Great Powers*
Ian Kershaw's *The "Hitler Myth": Image and Reality in the Third Reich*
John Maynard Keynes's *The General Theory of Employment, Interest and Money*
Charles P. Kindleberger's *Manias, Panics and Crashes*
Martin Luther King Jr's *Why We Can't Wait*
Henry Kissinger's *World Order: Reflections on the Character of Nations and the Course of History*
Thomas Kuhn's *The Structure of Scientific Revolutions*
Georges Lefebvre's *The Coming of the French Revolution*
John Locke's *Two Treatises of Government*
Niccolò Machiavelli's *The Prince*
Thomas Robert Malthus's *An Essay on the Principle of Population*
Mahmood Mamdani's *Citizen and Subject: Contemporary Africa And The Legacy Of Late Colonialism*
Karl Marx's *Capital*
Stanley Milgram's *Obedience to Authority*
John Stuart Mill's *On Liberty*
Thomas Paine's *Common Sense*
Thomas Paine's *Rights of Man*
Geoffrey Parker's *Global Crisis: War, Climate Change and Catastrophe in the Seventeenth Century*
Jonathan Riley-Smith's *The First Crusade and the Idea of Crusading*
Jean-Jacques Rousseau's *The Social Contract*
Joan Wallach Scott's *Gender and the Politics of History*
Theda Skocpol's *States and Social Revolutions*
Adam Smith's *The Wealth of Nations*
Timothy Snyder's *Bloodlands: Europe Between Hitler and Stalin*
Sun Tzu's *The Art of War*
Keith Thomas's *Religion and the Decline of Magic*
Thucydides's *The History of the Peloponnesian War*
Frederick Jackson Turner's *The Significance of the Frontier in American History*
Odd Arne Westad's *The Global Cold War: Third World Interventions And The Making Of Our Times*

The Macat Library By Discipline

LITERATURE

Chinua Achebe's *An Image of Africa: Racism in Conrad's Heart of Darkness*
Roland Barthes's *Mythologies*
Homi K. Bhabha's *The Location of Culture*
Judith Butler's *Gender Trouble*
Simone De Beauvoir's *The Second Sex*
Ferdinand De Saussure's *Course in General Linguistics*
T. S. Eliot's *The Sacred Wood: Essays on Poetry and Criticism*
Zora Neale Huston's *Characteristics of Negro Expression*
Toni Morrison's *Playing in the Dark: Whiteness in the American Literary Imagination*
Edward Said's *Orientalism*
Gayatri Chakravorty Spivak's *Can the Subaltern Speak?*
Mary Wollstonecraft's *A Vindication of the Rights of Women*
Virginia Woolf's *A Room of One's Own*

PHILOSOPHY

Elizabeth Anscombe's *Modern Moral Philosophy*
Hannah Arendt's *The Human Condition*
Aristotle's *Metaphysics*
Aristotle's *Nicomachean Ethics*
Edmund Gettier's *Is Justified True Belief Knowledge?*
Georg Wilhelm Friedrich Hegel's *Phenomenology of Spirit*
David Hume's *Dialogues Concerning Natural Religion*
David Hume's *The Enquiry for Human Understanding*
Immanuel Kant's *Religion within the Boundaries of Mere Reason*
Immanuel Kant's *Critique of Pure Reason*
Søren Kierkegaard's *The Sickness Unto Death*
Søren Kierkegaard's *Fear and Trembling*
C. S. Lewis's *The Abolition of Man*
Alasdair MacIntyre's *After Virtue*
Marcus Aurelius's *Meditations*
Friedrich Nietzsche's *On the Genealogy of Morality*
Friedrich Nietzsche's *Beyond Good and Evil*
Plato's *Republic*
Plato's *Symposium*
Jean-Jacques Rousseau's *The Social Contract*
Gilbert Ryle's *The Concept of Mind*
Baruch Spinoza's *Ethics*
Sun Tzu's *The Art of War*
Ludwig Wittgenstein's *Philosophical Investigations*

POLITICS

Benedict Anderson's *Imagined Communities*
Aristotle's *Politics*
Bernard Bailyn's *The Ideological Origins of the American Revolution*
Edmund Burke's *Reflections on the Revolution in France*
John C. Calhoun's *A Disquisition on Government*
Ha-Joon Chang's *Kicking Away the Ladder*
Hamid Dabashi's *Iran: A People Interrupted*
Hamid Dabashi's *Theology of Discontent: The Ideological Foundation of the Islamic Revolution in Iran*
Robert Dahl's *Democracy and its Critics*
Robert Dahl's *Who Governs?*
David Brion Davis's *The Problem of Slavery in the Age of Revolution*

Alexis De Tocqueville's *Democracy in America*
James Ferguson's *The Anti-Politics Machine*
Frank Dikotter's *Mao's Great Famine*
Sheila Fitzpatrick's *Everyday Stalinism*
Eric Foner's *Reconstruction: America's Unfinished Revolution, 1863-1877*
Milton Friedman's *Capitalism and Freedom*
Francis Fukuyama's *The End of History and the Last Man*
John Lewis Gaddis's *We Now Know: Rethinking Cold War History*
Ernest Gellner's *Nations and Nationalism*
David Graeber's *Debt: the First 5000 Years*
Antonio Gramsci's *The Prison Notebooks*
Alexander Hamilton, John Jay & James Madison's *The Federalist Papers*
Friedrich Hayek's *The Road to Serfdom*
Christopher Hill's *The World Turned Upside Down*
Thomas Hobbes's *Leviathan*
John A. Hobson's *Imperialism: A Study*
Samuel P. Huntington's *The Clash of Civilizations and the Remaking of World Order*
Tony Judt's *Postwar: A History of Europe Since 1945*
David C. Kang's *China Rising: Peace, Power and Order in East Asia*
Paul Kennedy's *The Rise and Fall of Great Powers*
Robert Keohane's *After Hegemony*
Martin Luther King Jr.'s *Why We Can't Wait*
Henry Kissinger's *World Order: Reflections on the Character of Nations and the Course of History*
John Locke's *Two Treatises of Government*
Niccolò Machiavelli's *The Prince*
Thomas Robert Malthus's *An Essay on the Principle of Population*
Mahmood Mamdani's *Citizen and Subject: Contemporary Africa And The Legacy Of Late Colonialism*
Karl Marx's *Capital*
John Stuart Mill's *On Liberty*
John Stuart Mill's *Utilitarianism*
Hans Morgenthau's *Politics Among Nations*
Thomas Paine's *Common Sense*
Thomas Paine's *Rights of Man*
Thomas Piketty's *Capital in the Twenty-First Century*
Robert D. Putman's *Bowling Alone*
John Rawls's *Theory of Justice*
Jean-Jacques Rousseau's *The Social Contract*
Theda Skocpol's *States and Social Revolutions*
Adam Smith's *The Wealth of Nations*
Sun Tzu's *The Art of War*
Henry David Thoreau's *Civil Disobedience*
Thucydides's *The History of the Peloponnesian War*
Kenneth Waltz's *Theory of International Politics*
Max Weber's *Politics as a Vocation*
Odd Arne Westad's *The Global Cold War: Third World Interventions And The Making Of Our Times*

POSTCOLONIAL STUDIES

Roland Barthes's *Mythologies*
Frantz Fanon's *Black Skin, White Masks*
Homi K. Bhabha's *The Location of Culture*
Gustavo Gutiérrez's *A Theology of Liberation*
Edward Said's *Orientalism*
Gayatri Chakravorty Spivak's *Can the Subaltern Speak?*

The Macat Library By Discipline

PSYCHOLOGY

Gordon Allport's *The Nature of Prejudice*
Alan Baddeley & Graham Hitch's *Aggression: A Social Learning Analysis*
Albert Bandura's *Aggression: A Social Learning Analysis*
Leon Festinger's *A Theory of Cognitive Dissonance*
Sigmund Freud's *The Interpretation of Dreams*
Betty Friedan's *The Feminine Mystique*
Michael R. Gottfredson & Travis Hirschi's *A General Theory of Crime*
Eric Hoffer's *The True Believer: Thoughts on the Nature of Mass Movements*
William James's *Principles of Psychology*
Elizabeth Loftus's *Eyewitness Testimony*
A. H. Maslow's *A Theory of Human Motivation*
Stanley Milgram's *Obedience to Authority*
Steven Pinker's *The Better Angels of Our Nature*
Oliver Sacks's *The Man Who Mistook His Wife For a Hat*
Richard Thaler & Cass Sunstein's *Nudge: Improving Decisions About Health, Wealth and Happiness*
Amos Tversky's *Judgment under Uncertainty: Heuristics and Biases*
Philip Zimbardo's *The Lucifer Effect*

SCIENCE

Rachel Carson's *Silent Spring*
William Cronon's *Nature's Metropolis: Chicago And The Great West*
Alfred W. Crosby's *The Columbian Exchange*
Charles Darwin's *On the Origin of Species*
Richard Dawkin's *The Selfish Gene*
Thomas Kuhn's *The Structure of Scientific Revolutions*
Geoffrey Parker's *Global Crisis: War, Climate Change and Catastrophe in the Seventeenth Century*
Mathis Wackernagel & William Rees's *Our Ecological Footprint*

SOCIOLOGY

Michelle Alexander's *The New Jim Crow: Mass Incarceration in the Age of Colorblindness*
Gordon Allport's *The Nature of Prejudice*
Albert Bandura's *Aggression: A Social Learning Analysis*
Hanna Batatu's *The Old Social Classes And The Revolutionary Movements Of Iraq*
Ha-Joon Chang's *Kicking Away the Ladder*
W. E. B. Du Bois's *The Souls of Black Folk*
Émile Durkheim's *On Suicide*
Frantz Fanon's *Black Skin, White Masks*
Frantz Fanon's *The Wretched of the Earth*
Eric Foner's *Reconstruction: America's Unfinished Revolution, 1863-1877*
Eugene Genovese's *Roll, Jordan, Roll: The World the Slaves Made*
Jack Goldstone's *Revolution and Rebellion in the Early Modern World*
Antonio Gramsci's *The Prison Notebooks*
Richard Herrnstein & Charles A Murray's *The Bell Curve: Intelligence and Class Structure in American Life*
Eric Hoffer's *The True Believer: Thoughts on the Nature of Mass Movements*
Jane Jacobs's *The Death and Life of Great American Cities*
Robert Lucas's *Why Doesn't Capital Flow from Rich to Poor Countries?*
Jay Macleod's *Ain't No Makin' It: Aspirations and Attainment in a Low Income Neighborhood*
Elaine May's *Homeward Bound: American Families in the Cold War Era*
Douglas McGregor's *The Human Side of Enterprise*
C. Wright Mills's *The Sociological Imagination*

Thomas Piketty's *Capital in the Twenty-First Century*
Robert D. Putman's *Bowling Alone*
David Riesman's *The Lonely Crowd: A Study of the Changing American Character*
Edward Said's *Orientalism*
Joan Wallach Scott's *Gender and the Politics of History*
Theda Skocpol's *States and Social Revolutions*
Max Weber's *The Protestant Ethic and the Spirit of Capitalism*

THEOLOGY

Augustine's *Confessions*
Benedict's *Rule of St Benedict*
Gustavo Gutiérrez's *A Theology of Liberation*
Carole Hillenbrand's *The Crusades: Islamic Perspectives*
David Hume's *Dialogues Concerning Natural Religion*
Immanuel Kant's *Religion within the Boundaries of Mere Reason*
Ernst Kantorowicz's *The King's Two Bodies: A Study in Medieval Political Theology*
Søren Kierkegaard's *The Sickness Unto Death*
C. S. Lewis's *The Abolition of Man*
Saba Mahmood's *The Politics of Piety: The Islamic Revival and the Feminist Subject*
Baruch Spinoza's *Ethics*
Keith Thomas's *Religion and the Decline of Magic*

COMING SOON

Chris Argyris's *The Individual and the Organisation*
Seyla Benhabib's *The Rights of Others*
Walter Benjamin's *The Work Of Art in the Age of Mechanical Reproduction*
John Berger's *Ways of Seeing*
Pierre Bourdieu's *Outline of a Theory of Practice*
Mary Douglas's *Purity and Danger*
Roland Dworkin's *Taking Rights Seriously*
James G. March's *Exploration and Exploitation in Organisational Learning*
Ikujiro Nonaka's *A Dynamic Theory of Organizational Knowledge Creation*
Griselda Pollock's *Vision and Difference*
Amartya Sen's *Inequality Re-Examined*
Susan Sontag's *On Photography*
Yasser Tabbaa's *The Transformation of Islamic Art*
Ludwig von Mises's *Theory of Money and Credit*

Macat Disciplines

Access the greatest ideas and thinkers across entire disciplines, including

Postcolonial Studies

Roland Barthes's *Mythologies*
Frantz Fanon's *Black Skin, White Masks*
Homi K. Bhabha's *The Location of Culture*
Gustavo Gutiérrez's *A Theology of Liberation*
Edward Said's *Orientalism*
Gayatri Chakravorty Spivak's *Can the Subaltern Speak?*

Macat analyses are available from all good bookshops and libraries.

Access hundreds of analyses through one, multimedia tool.
Join free for one month **library.macat.com**

Macat Disciplines

Access the greatest ideas and thinkers across entire disciplines, including

MACAT

AFRICANA STUDIES

Chinua Achebe's *An Image of Africa: Racism in Conrad's Heart of Darkness*

W. E. B. Du Bois's *The Souls of Black Folk*

Zora Neale Hurston's *Characteristics of Negro Expression*

Martin Luther King Jr.'s *Why We Can't Wait*

Toni Morrison's *Playing in the Dark: Whiteness in the American Literary Imagination*

Macat analyses are available from all good bookshops and libraries.

Access hundreds of analyses through one, multimedia tool.
Join free for one month **library.macat.com**

Macat Pairs

Analyse historical and modern issues from opposite sides of an argument. Pairs include:

MACAT

MACAT

ARE WE FUNDAMENTALLY GOOD - OR BAD?

Steven Pinker's
The Better Angels of Our Nature

Stephen Pinker's gloriously optimistic 2011 book argues that, despite humanity's biological tendency toward violence, we are, in fact, less violent today than ever before. To prove his case, Pinker lays out pages of detailed statistical evidence. For him, much of the credit for the decline goes to the eighteenth-century Enlightenment movement, whose ideas of liberty, tolerance, and respect for the value of human life filtered down through society and affected how people thought. That psychological change led to behavioral change—and overall we became more peaceful. Critics countered that humanity could never overcome the biological urge toward violence; others argued that Pinker's statistics were flawed.

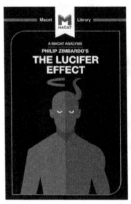

Philip Zimbardo's
The Lucifer Effect

Some psychologists believe those who commit cruelty are innately evil. Zimbardo disagrees. In *The Lucifer Effect*, he argues that sometimes good people do evil things simply because of the situations they find themselves in, citing many historical examples to illustrate his point. Zimbardo details his 1971 Stanford prison experiment, where ordinary volunteers playing guards in a mock prison rapidly became abusive. But he also describes the tortures committed by US army personnel in Iraq's Abu Ghraib prison in 2003—and how he himself testified in defence of one of those guards. committed by US army personnel in Iraq's Abu Ghraib prison in 2003—and how he himself testified in defence of one of those guards.

Macat analyses are available from all good bookshops and libraries.

Access hundreds of analyses through one, multimedia tool.
Join free for one month **library.macat.com**

Macat Pairs

Analyse historical and modern issues from opposite sides of an argument. Pairs include:

RACE AND IDENTITY

Zora Neale Hurston's
Characteristics of Negro Expression

Using material collected on anthropological expeditions to the South, Zora Neale Hurston explains how expression in African American culture in the early twentieth century departs from the art of white America. At the time, African American art was often criticized for copying white culture. For Hurston, this criticism misunderstood how art works. European tradition views art as something fixed. But Hurston describes a creative process that is alive, ever-changing, and largely improvisational. She maintains that African American art works through a process called 'mimicry'—where an imitated object or verbal pattern, for example, is reshaped and altered until it becomes something new, novel—and worthy of attention.

Frantz Fanon's
Black Skin, White Masks

Black Skin, White Masks offers a radical analysis of the psychological effects of colonization on the colonized.

Fanon witnessed the effects of colonization first hand both in his birthplace, Martinique, and again later in life when he worked as a psychiatrist in another French colony, Algeria. His text is uncompromising in form and argument. He dissects the dehumanizing effects of colonialism, arguing that it destroys the native sense of identity, forcing people to adapt to an alien set of values—including a core belief that they are inferior. This results in deep psychological trauma.

Fanon's work played a pivotal role in the civil rights movements of the 1960s.

Macat analyses are available from all good bookshops and libraries.

Access hundreds of analyses through one, multimedia tool.
Join free for one month **library.macat.com**

Macat Disciplines

Access the greatest ideas and thinkers across entire disciplines, including

INEQUALITY

Ha-Joon Chang's, *Kicking Away the Ladder*

David Graeber's, *Debt: The First 5000 Years*

Robert E. Lucas's, *Why Doesn't Capital Flow from Rich To Poor Countries?*

Thomas Piketty's, *Capital in the Twenty-First Century*

Amartya Sen's, *Inequality Re-Examined*

Mahbub Ul Haq's, *Reflections on Human Development*

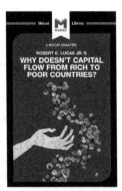

Macat analyses are available from all good bookshops and libraries.

Access hundreds of analyses through one, multimedia tool.
Join free for one month **library.macat.com**

Macat Disciplines

*Access the greatest ideas and thinkers
across entire disciplines, including*

CRIMINOLOGY

Michelle Alexander's
*The New Jim Crow:
Mass Incarceration in the
Age of Colorblindness*

**Michael R. Gottfredson
& Travis Hirschi's**
A General Theory of Crime

Elizabeth Loftus's
Eyewitness Testimony

**Richard Herrnstein
& Charles A. Murray's**
*The Bell Curve: Intelligence and
Class Structure in American Life*

Jay Macleod's
*Ain't No Makin' It:
Aspirations and Attainment in a
Low-Income Neighborhood*

Philip Zimbardo's
The Lucifer Effect

Macat analyses are available from all good bookshops and libraries.

Access hundreds of analyses through one, multimedia tool.
Join free for one month **library.macat.com**